Reflections

# In Sweet Obscurity
## Learning from Some of the Bible's Lesser-Known Saints

Kurt Strassner

DayOne

Unless stated otherwise, all Scripture quotations are taken from the New American Standard Bible®, Copyright © 1960, 1962, 1963, 1968, 1971, 1972, 1973, 1975, 1977, 1995 by The Lockman Foundation. Used by permission. (www.Lockman.org)
Scripture quotations marked NIV are taken from the Holy Bible, New International Version®, NIV®. Copyright © 1973, 1978, 1984, 2011 by Biblica, Inc.™ Used by permission of Zondervan. All rights reserved worldwide. www.zondervan.com. The 'NIV' and 'New International Version' are trademarks registered in the United States Patent and Trademark Office by Biblica, Inc.™.

British Library Cataloguing in Publication Data available

ISBN 978-1-84625-540-3


Published by Day One Publications
Ryelands Road, Leominster, HR6 8NZ

☎ 01568 613 740
FAX: 01568 611 473
email—sales@dayone.co.uk
web site—www.dayone.co.uk

Cover designed by Rob Jones, Elk Design
Printed by TJ International Ltd.

For
Julia, Andrew, Silas, Salome, Elisabeth, and Levi—
all named after lesser-known (but faithful!)
men and women of the Bible.
May God grant that your testimonies,
whether in the limelight or in the shadows,
may be as heartening as theirs.

With many thanks to editor Suzanne Mitchell, who has patiently helped me through this and other projects.

# Endorsements

*In this valuable little book Kurt Strassner has opened up the stories of some fascinating but lesser-known Bible personalities. With true expository skill, warm pastoral concern, and a helpful clear structure to each chapter, he brings out the hidden qualities of each character, as well as the many important principles and compelling applications which can be derived from each account. The book is, above all, a powerful pointer to the spectacular providence of God as he works to bring about his perfect plan, often in the most hidden of people and places. It will be a huge encouragement to ordinary Christians who are tempted to think that their lives don't matter.*

**Iver Martin, Principal, Edinburgh Theological Seminary**

*Most of us won't be read about or even heard of in a generation or two. Perhaps you can't remember even a single notable action of your great-grandfather. But he lived and, if he was a believer, he had important work to do. Kurt Strassner gives us 'lesser knowns' durable encouragement. We forget that it doesn't make any difference if we're headliners in God's work, so long as we are faithful. Read to learn how to live 'In Sweet Obscurity'.*

**Jim Elliff, Christian Communicators Worldwide**

# Contents

# Introduction

Be honest now: When you opened to this book's Contents page, did you immediately recognize the names that head each chapter—Ebed-melech, Obadiah, Epaphras, and so on? Don't feel bad if the answer is 'no'; this book has been a learning experience for me too! Allow me to tell you how it came about.

It was a Friday evening and I had no sermon. Not only did I have no *sermon*, I did not even have a *passage* in mind from which to write a sermon! And, as I sometimes do at times like this, I had allowed myself to become quite discouraged. But then, during our family devotions that evening, we read the story of a little-known palace servant named Obadiah in 1 Kings 18 (see Chapter 2 to follow).[1] In a time of great persecution, he protected God's prophets by hiding them in caves and shielding them from the ruthlessness of the pagan queen, Jezebel. Reading his story, I was so moved that, before I went to sleep that night, a sermon had already begun to write itself in my mind! Praise God for his faithfulness!

The next day, I sat down to begin scribbling down my thoughts. I was hoping just to get through this *one* sermon and this one weekend, and then have another go, on Monday morning, at figuring out what the next *series* of sermons should be. But, as I studied and jotted down notes from the account of this obscure Old Testament saint, it occurred to me that the next series of sermons might actually be beginning, right then and there, on the yellow legal pad resting on my lap. I was receiving a great deal of joy studying this minor character called Obadiah—learning from his example, admiring his courage, and so on. So much so that I thought that perhaps I (along with my congregation) would enjoy and benefit from taking a look at a handful of similar such passages and people: men and women of the Bible who are little known to *us*, but whose names and faithfulness are surely known and recognized in the courts of heaven.

'Minor characters can be very important in God's grand scheme of things,' I began writing in my notes. For instance, not many people know about this courageous man called Obadiah. Not many parents name their sons after him. He was very much a bit player in God's great plan for the ages. He comes briefly onto the stage of biblical history in 1 Kings 18, and then he disappears back into the shadows of obscurity. He is the epitome of a minor character. Yet how important was Obadiah to the hundred prophets he kept alive in a cave during a time of great persecution (1 Kings 18:3–4)? How important was he to their wives and children? And how valuable was Obadiah to the flocks of believers who were fed by the ministry of these hundred men? Perhaps thousands of people were later blessed with the word of God by the preaching ministry of these one hundred prophets. But that was only possible because this one courageous man had hidden them in a cave and brought them daily rations! So, for untold numbers of people, Obadiah's minor part in the Bible's storyline was of major significance! Indeed, for those people, his value was simply incalculable!

More importantly, how valuable was Obadiah to God himself? After all, it was *his* word and *his* honour that were at stake in those dark days in Israel. So there is no doubt that *God* took note of Obadiah's courage and faith. For, remember, 'The eyes of the LORD are in every place, watching the evil and the good' (Prov. 15:3). So of course he was watching Obadiah as he hustled food out to those caves! He's always watching— even the minor characters and bit actors!

These are the thoughts that were pulsating in my mind and heart that Saturday evening as I studied a biblical hero I had taken little notice of up until that point. When you read Chapter 2 of this book you will, Lord willing, see even more reasons to value this relatively unknown man called Obadiah. Moreover, it is my hope that that experience will repeat itself in each chapter that lies ahead. All these pages are devoted to gleaning encouragements from stories and people whom you may have little noticed before. But how outstanding these men and women were! How honoured by their heavenly Father! Indeed, it is remarkable to observe how many minor characters are honoured in the pages of Scripture. The Bible is filled with all sorts of names that we do not know (and often cannot pronounce!) but that are well known to God. He has them all recorded in his books, even if we have overlooked or forgotten them.

For instance, there was Mr what's-his-name who helped the prophet Jeremiah out of a miry pit, and sent down some old T-shirts 'to pad the ropes' (Jer. 38:12, NIV) and keep Jeremiah's armpits from being rubbed raw. *We* may not recall his story, but *God* has it all written down! Or what about the old man who met David while he was fleeing from his son Absalom, and provided his men with food, bedding, and so on? What was his name again? God knows! And he knows all the other characters, large and small, in between! We may not remember them; perhaps we've not yet even discovered them. But to Jeremiah, and to David, and to the prophets hidden in the caves, how invaluable they were! And how precious these no-name saints are in the sight of their heavenly Father!

These thoughts alone ought to be an encouragement to us—before we ever study any of these men and women close up. For almost every one of us is a minor character. There are a handful of Christian leaders alive today whose names will go down in the history books and whose writings will still be in print a hundred years from now. But you and I are probably not in their number. Perhaps our families will at least remember our names a century from now. But, otherwise, we will all largely be forgotten to history by the year 2116. But we won't be forgotten by *God*, no matter how small our parts in his story! 'The eyes of the LORD are in every place, watching'! So you can rest assured that he sees *you*, however minor your role!

God sees and takes note when you fear him more than you fear your boss, or your co-workers, or that unbelieving family member who seems to have it in for you because of your faith in Jesus. He has his pen in hand as he watches you serve in the children's Sunday school, or as you visit the elderly, or as you pray for your church's missionaries. All these things are written in his books, just like the deeds of obscure Obadiah!

Moreover, how valuable will your work in Sunday school be to those children who will someday be in heaven because of it? How precious will your seemingly small efforts be to those neighbours who will someday love and treasure Jesus because of your witness to them? How important are you to those missionaries who survive the disappointments and difficulties of the foreign field leaning on your prayers? The answers are simply incalculable! So take heart, you who feel as if your attempts to serve the Lord do not amount to anything great. Go on playing your minor parts to the glory of God. The great day will prove that it was all worth it! I hope that the stories and encouragements in the pages that follow will do the same. Enjoy!

# Barzillai:

## Eighty years old
### … and still useful

*Now when David had come to Mahanaim, Shobi the son of Nahash from Rabbah of the sons of Ammon, Machir the son of Ammiel from Lo-debar, and Barzillai the Gileadite from Rogelim, brought beds, basins, pottery, wheat, barley, flour, parched grain, beans, lentils, parched seeds, honey, curds, sheep, and cheese of the herd, for David and for the people who were with him, to eat; for they said, 'The people are hungry and weary and thirsty in the wilderness.'*

*(2 Sam. 17:27–29)*

It was no mirage: over the barren horizon came a rumbling herd of sheep and servants, carts and camels, sacks and crates—all loaded down with supplies! What manna in the wilderness these provisions must have been to David and his exhausted men—especially at such a painful moment in the king's life! David was out in that lonely countryside because his son Absalom had set in motion a military operation to overthrow his father and grab the throne for himself. Things eventually got so bad that David and many of his supporters had to flee Jerusalem and find refuge in the wilderness.

These were sad days. God's anointed king had become a fugitive from his own son—barefoot and weeping, leading a bedraggled band of supporters into the wilds across the Jordan River. But this was not the only caravan on the move that day. Making their way down to meet David were three men whose names are easily forgotten by us, but surely not by David. Were it not for the kindness of Shobi, Machir, and Barzillai, David and his band might have been swallowed up, either by the barren wilderness or by the armies of Absalom. Instead, the king's men, sustained by the generosity of this unheralded trio, were eventually able (in 2 Sam. 18) to beat back Absalom's attacking forces, to quash the rebellion, and (in ch. 19) to begin making their way back towards Jerusalem. And, as they approached the Jordan River on their way home, one of the three, Barzillai, was there again—this time, not with supplies, but with much-needed encouragement and companionship for his friend and king:

> Now Barzillai the Gileadite had come down from Rogelim; and he went on to the Jordan with the king to escort him over the Jordan. Now Barzillai was very old, being eighty years old; and he had sustained the king while he stayed at Mahanaim, for he was a very great man. The king said to Barzillai, 'You cross over with me and I will sustain you in Jerusalem with me.' But Barzillai said to the king, 'How long have I yet to live, that I should go up with the king to Jerusalem? I am now eighty years old. Can I distinguish between good and bad? Or can your servant taste what I eat or what I drink? Or can I hear anymore the voice of singing men and women? Why then should your servant be an added burden to my lord the king? Your servant would merely cross over the Jordan with the king. Why should the king compensate me with this reward? Please let your servant return, that I may die in my own city near the grave of my father and my mother' … The king

then kissed Barzillai and blessed him, and he returned
to his place.

(2 Sam. 19:31–37, 39)

Many are the lessons this saintly old man could teach
us! We will focus, however, on only three. Firstly, Barzillai
reminds us of …

### The purpose of wealth

Sometimes in my family we joke about how, on holidays,
our grandmothers used to prepare enough food to feed an
army. Hyperbole, to be sure! But Barzillai, Shobi, and Machir
actually did it! They brought enough beans, lentils, flour,
sheep, honey, cheese, and so on, literally to feed an army of
hundreds of men! So they must have been men of considerable
means. As we are told in 19:32, Barzillai was 'a very great man'.
He was a man of no small importance, no small character, and
no small financial resources!

But what was the *purpose* of all that wealth? Why had God
given Barzillai such deep pockets? So he could curry favour
with the king, or make a name for himself? No. We read in
chapter 19 that he had no interest in joining the king's court,
or in being repaid from the king's coffers. Rather, he preferred
to stay in his own home town—an apparent backwater that
is never mentioned anywhere else in the Bible: Rogelim. So if
Barzillai did not possess such deep pockets in order to become
politically or personally powerful and important, why did
God allow him such affluence? Very simply, so that he might

be generous to David and his men. That is the purpose of wealth—generosity!

It is not necessarily a bad thing to be wealthy. In fact, if wealth comes as a blessing from God to an honest, hard-working individual, it can be a positively good thing. How different would the story of Jesus be, for instance, if there had been no one in Jerusalem wealthy enough to have a large upper room where the Lord and his disciples might enjoy their last supper? Or if certain Jewish women had not been financially secure enough to help fund Jesus and his disciples' preaching tours 'out of their private means' (Luke 8:3)?

There are all sorts of godly people in the Bible who possessed great wealth, and had the possessions to match. Barzillai was among them. Though he lived in a small town, we should probably not picture him living in a ramshackle cottage. Surely it was from a sprawling ranch that all those dairy, grain, and meat products came! In addition, he must have had a considerable number of servants to help him carry those cartloads over hill and valley to David's men. Barzillai was rich! And the Bible does not condemn Barzillai for having such assets at his disposal. But what the Bible does do—in the cases of Barzillai, of the women who financially supported Jesus, and of the family with the upper room in Jerusalem—is show how these people were willing to use their affluence on behalf of people in need, and especially on behalf of *God's* people in need.

God gives us wealth so that we might use it on behalf of other people, and especially in the advancement of his kingdom. So let's not condemn ourselves for that which God has given us as his blessing; but let's also not use his blessings simply on ourselves. Rather, let us, like Barzillai, hold on to our money and possessions with very loose fingers—always willing for them to be used by, and even given to, people who need them far more than we do!

Think about how much it must have cost to sustain David's men for all those days. Beds, cookware, food, sheep, and so on—those things add up when multiplied by hundreds of soldiers! But Barzillai was willing to part with it all for David's sake, and for the sake of David's kingdom and David's God.

We should note that last sentence well. In doing *David* good, Barzillai did the *entire kingdom* good. For, as the king prospered or suffered, so did all of his subjects. And the kingdom, of course, was not just David's kingdom, but God's. So Barzillai used his wealth, not just for a few hundred soldiers, but for the welfare of the entire kingdom of God's people! Shouldn't we, who serve that kingdom in much fuller flower, be willing to do the same? So we must always have our eyes and ears open, asking God to show us how we might use our wealth (however great or small) for the sake of those in need, and for the sake of the kingdom of Christ.

In Barzillai's generosity, we see the purpose of wealth. But, secondly, he also shows us …

### The possibilities of old age
When Barzillai saved the day for David and his frazzled

companions, he was no less than eighty years old! Yes, it is true that Old Testament saints often seem to have aged at quite a different rate from you and I. For instance, Moses' great work did not begin until he was eighty years old—and he lived and served for another four decades after that! I don't see that happening for me! And then there was Caleb. At age eighty-five, he claimed he was still as strong as at the age of forty! So the fact is that many early Old Testament men and women seem to have lived a lot longer and stronger than we do—and to have aged at a much slower rate.

But this was emphatically *not* the case with Barzillai. He was not like Moses or Caleb in this respect. The narrator of 2 Samuel, in fact, makes a point of calling him 'very old' (19:32). Along those lines, notice that Barzillai himself did not at all speak with the confidence and testosterone of Caleb! Caleb, in his eighties, felt as strong as ever. But old Barzillai spoke like this in 19:35: 'I am now eighty years old. Can I distinguish between good and bad? Or can your servant taste what I eat or what I drink? Or can I hear anymore the voice of singing men and women? Why then should your servant be an added burden to my lord the king?'

That sounds more like the way older people usually talk, doesn't it? 'I feel that I am such a burden. My mind is going. I can't taste anything any more. And, if I don't have my hearing aid in, I have a really hard time following along with the singing at church.' That was Barzillai. Yet, even at that age and with those infirmities, he was still trekking across the wilderness to serve the Lord! And what that reminds us of, very simply, is that old age does not mean uselessness in God's kingdom.

Maybe you are there already. In fact, perhaps even now you are feeling sympathy pains as you think of Barzillai travelling all that way (either on foot or on the back of a donkey) to meet David in the wilderness. Those of us who are not so old will understand soon; the challenges of old age will come more quickly than we think. And, when they do, there will be great encouragement for us in the pages of 2 Samuel 17 and 19!

Barzillai's name is scarcely mentioned in the pages of the Bible outside these two chapters. So it may well be that his greatest service for the Lord occurred right there in the wilderness … at age eighty! In other words, he did his greatest work when his hearing was all but gone; when his taste buds were as good as dead; and when his mind was so often confused that he felt no longer able to 'distinguish between good and bad'. The lesson? Old age, the autumn of life, can actually be a season of great opportunity! If Barzillai could be so useful when he actually felt like a 'burden', then you and I may be, too.

It is true that, at eighty, you will no longer be able to do what you did when you were thirty. No doubt Barzillai himself—perhaps even with a note of sadness—realized the turn of events that five decades of life had brought on. Had he been thirty instead of eighty, he would probably have been out in the fields fighting valiantly with David's soldiers rather than stocking the canteen back at base camp. But remember this as well: had Barzillai been thirty instead of eighty, it's quite possible he would not yet have accumulated the resources necessary for feeding an army of men—and David and his men, therefore, may have had no strength to fight in the first place! So the eighty-year-old, back with the supply wagons, was indispensible to the military victory. And God's providence so often works in exactly this way.

There is no debating the fact that strength, mental agility, endurance, and so many useful capacities are available to thirty-year-olds in measures that senior citizens can only remember fondly. But it is also true that wisdom, accumulated wealth, and free time (for service, and especially for prayer) are often available to older men and women in ways the young can only dream about wistfully. So let us not feel useless because we cannot do what others can, or what we once did. But let us, when we are old, see that with our old age comes the opportunity to serve God in ways we never could before; and perhaps in ways that no one else in the church has time or money to do.

Barzillai served God well into his 'retirement years'. And he did so, notably, with a keen understanding of …

## The logic of humility

Note well Barzillai's response in chapter 19 to David's offer to bring him to Jerusalem and to support him from the king's coffers. Barzillai gave three reasons for declining the invitation. Firstly, he was old (v. 35), and he felt he would be a burden to the king. Also, like a lot of older folk, he was not keen on the idea of leaving his home after all those years in one place (v. 37). But there is another noteworthy reason why Barzillai did not go and receive a hero's welcome in Jerusalem: because he did not feel much like a hero! Isn't that what he was getting at in verse 36? 'Your servant would merely cross over the Jordan with the king. Why should the king compensate me with this reward?'

Why would Barzillai have said that? Why didn't he expect a reward from the king? The fact that Barzillai (in the quote above, and three other times in this passage) refers to himself as David's 'servant' gives us an important hint. What do servants do? They serve. So of course Barzillai had brought food and bedding to the king: it was simply his duty as the king's 'servant'. And he did not seem to imagine that he deserved any great reward for merely doing his duty. Yes, he *allowed* David to pass along the blessing to one Chimham (vv. 37–38), but he saw no reason to *expect* such compensation.

Should this not be *our* attitude when we serve *our* Lord and King? As we will see in a later chapter, our heavenly king is indeed 'a rewarder of those who seek Him' (Heb. 11:6)—just as King David desired to be for Barzillai. Such an attitude befits the office of a king! But the logic that exists in the minds of us, *the servants*, ought surely to be along the same lines as that of Barzillai: 'Why should the king compensate *me* with this reward?'[1] 'What have *I* done to deserve all this? I am simply the king's servant ... and at his service.'

Shouldn't that be our heartbeat with our God? Yes, many

of God's faithful people give generously to his work, much like Barzillai. And it is not wrong to look forward to God's reward for our faithfulness (see Matt. 6:4, for instance). But, at the end of the day, do humble people think they *deserve* to see their names posted in heaven among a list of 'platinum donors'? Of course not! Indeed, we might rather be almost embarrassed to see such a thing (in heaven or on earth), because 'we have done only that which we ought to have done' (Luke 17:10). We have done only what is expected of the King's servants. That seems to have been Barzillai's attitude towards the king and his reward. That is the logic of servants and kings—a logic of humility.

Are *you* one of the King's servants? Have you come to bow the knee to Christ as your sovereign? One of the ways in which you will be able to tell is if you have begun to think of yourself like Barzillai before *his* king—simply as his 'servant'. I do encourage you to bow the knee in this way: to serve the Lord Jesus as your King! For has *he* not so well served *you*? Barzillai *brought* sheep—probably a whole flock of them—to be slaughtered for their meat so as to preserve the lives of David and his men in the wilderness. That was quite a gift! But in order to preserve *our* lives, Christ came into the wilderness of this fallen world in order to *be* 'the Lamb of God'—slain in order to take away our sin! Here is another reason we should be humble before him: because, in the gospel, the roles are reversed. In the gospel, the King washes the feet of the servants. In the gospel, the King becomes the servant of all. In the gospel, the King dies for his people! And if we have such a King—one who so loves us; one who has paid such a high price to purchase us as his own—can we call ourselves anything other than what Barzillai called himself, four times, in the presence of David? 'Lord, I humble myself before you. I am "your servant".'

Reflect on these points

1. *Are you wealthy? If you live in the Western world, the chances are that you are much more like Barzillai than like the widow in Luke 21, who possessed only 'two small copper coins'. How can you be like them both, in giving your wealth away to the Lord's work and people?*

2. *Do you consider yourself to be old? If so, has it occurred to you that God may still have your greatest kingdom work ahead of you? If you are not so old, how might you encourage those who are towards the usefulness that God intends for them?*

3. *Spend some time meditating on what it means to be a servant. God does reward his faithful people, and it is not wrong to look forward to his rewards. But have you begun to think that you deserve such things? Or, when he blesses you or grants you some recognition for your labours, is it your natural response to say with Barzillai, 'Why me?'*

# Obadiah:
## Man of courage

*Now Obadiah feared the LORD greatly; for when Jezebel destroyed the prophets of the LORD, Obadiah took a hundred prophets and hid them by fifties in a cave, and provided them with bread and water.*

*(1 Kings 18:3b–4)*

Queen Jezebel had grown up pagan. She was not an Israelite, but the daughter of a Canaanite king (1 Kings 16:29–33) and a worshipper of the Canaanite fertility god Baal. So, when King Ahab (fool that he was) married her and brought her into his palace in Israel, she seems to have had one very large goal in mind: she would promote the worship of Baal among the people of Israel (see the apparent connection between Ahab's marriage and his turning to Baal in 16:31; and Jezebel's support of the prophets of Baal in 18:19). In fact, Jezebel did not merely have in mind to *introduce* the worship of *Baal* in her new home country; she also made it her aim to *stamp out* the worship of *the one true God*. That is why we read in 18:4 that 'Jezebel destroyed the prophets of the LORD'. She wanted to get rid of God, and so she was bent on getting rid of his prophets. And she almost succeeded! But that is where this marvellous character Obadiah comes in. He was a royal official in the palace of Ahab (v. 3a); he was therefore privy to Jezebel's plans and decided he must do something about them. So he 'took a hundred prophets and hid them by fifties in a cave, and provided them with bread and water'.

Think for a moment about the courage this must have required. It would involve significant bravery to stand up to *any* queen, anywhere—but especially this queen! Jezebel had already shown that she was more than willing to destroy innocent people in order to get her way. That is why Obadiah sprang into action in the first place—because Jezebel was so malevolent! So fearsome was this woman, in fact, that Elijah (arguably the greatest of the Old Testament prophets) fled for his life from her presence (1 Kings 19)! Yet *Obadiah* stood against her, and it must have required great courage to have done so! In undermining the queen's plan, Obadiah risked his career in Ahab's court. More than that, he risked his life! As we will see, Obadiah risked all these things for the sake of the word of the Lord.

This was a man of remarkable courage. So let us consider his courage, and God's record of it, under three headings. The first thing to notice is that, in the courage of Obadiah, we have a lesson concerning ...

### The fear of the Lord

As we read verse 4, we might imagine Obadiah having the courage of a superhero: as an incredibly brave, lion-like figure who could stand up against anything. But, if we read on in 1 Kings 18, we find that this wasn't exactly the case. Actually, Obadiah's knees knocked together as he thought about his subversion of the queen (vv. 13–14). He feared for his life—just as you or I would have done in the face of an Ahab and a Jezebel. But he acted anyway! He showed courage anyway!

What was his secret? How could Obadiah be so courageous

when, inside, he was afraid for his life? The key, I believe, is found in verse 3. We are never told that Obadiah was a naturally courageous man. We are never told that he did not fear the king and queen; the plain fact is that he did. But what we *are* told in verse 3 is that 'Obadiah feared *the* LORD' … evidently more than he feared *the king*, and more than he feared the king's tyrannical wife!

The fear of the Lord, I suggest, is the key to great courage. Having great courage does not mean that a man or woman has no fears. It does not mean that we never tremble at the thought of the difficulties that lie before us. Great courage simply means that we fear the Lord *more* than we fear the difficulties. That was the defining truth of Obadiah's actions. He feared the Lord so much that his fear of the queen took a back seat, and he was able to act. He was more afraid of dishonouring the Lord than he was of defying the queen. And you and I, by the same token, must be more afraid of dishonouring the Lord than of being laughed at for our faith. We must be more averse to disappointing God than we are to being called a fanatic or being persecuted for what we believe. That is courage: to fear God more than the queen; to fear God more than earthly difficulty and distress.

The simple truth is that all of us are going to be afraid from time to time. You may sense, for instance, that the Spirit is nudging you to venture out on a limb and share your faith with that co-worker, to risk being thought strange or impertinent by speaking the gospel truth. And something inside your stomach is going to begin to tremble. Or maybe you will be faced with the necessity of taking an ethical stand at your workplace in a situation in which you know that either you or your company stand to lose money if you do what is right. And you are going to wrestle in your soul about what to do. Or maybe the fear will come with your realization that you need to hold a brother in Christ accountable for some sin-problem in his life. And your heart is going to pound when you see him sitting a few seats down from you on Sunday morning.

The question in each of those situations is not whether you are afraid. Of course you are! The question is: Whom do you fear most? God, or your boss? God, or your co-worker? God, or man's opinions of you?

Obadiah's courage was *not* an indication that he was unafraid in the face of his trial. Rather, his courage was evidence that he *feared God* more than he *feared man*! Make no mistake, Obadiah feared Ahab and Jezebel. But he 'feared the Lord *greatly*'! And so must we.

In the second place, in the courage of Obadiah, we are given a reminder of …

### The value of the word of God

Queen Jezebel, remember, was determined to eradicate the worship of the God of Israel. But what was her strategy? How did she go about stamping out the worship of the one true God? Note well that she didn't get busy destroying *all* of God's worshippers. Nor did she necessarily target all the *high-ranking* followers of the Lord, such as Obadiah. Rather, what we are told in 1 Kings 18:4 is that she set her sights specifically on 'the prophets'. But why? Why the prophets and not everyone else? It wasn't because the prophets were inherently better than the rest of God's people, or even that they were necessarily more godly. As we all know, preachers are sinners just like everyone else, and in need of grace just like everyone else. So, on many levels, these men were no more valuable than any of the other followers of the Lord. But Jezebel singled them out for destruction. Why?

Remember that it was through the *prophets* of the Lord that the *word* of the Lord came to his people. It was through the prophets of the Lord that the people were informed, encouraged, convicted, and taught—all so that they might know *how* to worship God, and *why*; and so that they might actually be inspired by the preaching to do so. The prophets were the mouthpieces of God. So if Jezebel could silence them, the people would soon be scattered all over the place, spiritually. For they would have no one to teach them the truth and to guide them in it. That is surely why Jezebel wanted to kill the prophets. Eradicate them, and you eradicate the word of God. And, once you have eradicated the *word* of God, the *worship* of God will collapse by itself for its lack of foundation.

The word of God, through the prophets, was vital! That must be why Jezebel wanted to *destroy* them … and why Obadiah wanted to *save* them. He was protecting, not just men, but the word of God through those men. That is why he

29

was willing to lose his job and even his life—because the word of God was at stake in the lives of these hundred prophets.

Think also, not just about *the risk* Obadiah took, but also about *the monumental size of the task* that lay before him. He was providing food for a hundred people—and he wasn't doing it in a nice church kitchen! He wasn't cooking over a nice stove, and then passing shiny food trays through a serving window to the people. That is hard enough work, isn't it? Those who help prepare the fellowship meals in church will say 'Amen'! Feeding a hundred people in any context requires a good deal of sweat. But Obadiah (and whatever helpers were with him) had not only to prepare the food … but then to carry it out into the fields and to the caves … and to do so secretly … and then perhaps to do it all again the next day, and the day after that! And who knows how long all of this went on!

Consider *the financial aspect* of this ministry as well. We do not know for sure where Obadiah got the funding for this giant food project. Perhaps he finagled a way to use government funds to help these men. After all, it was God's money in the king's coffers, was it not? But it is also possible, given the covert nature of his doings, that Obadiah had to pay for all that 'bread and water' out of his own pocket, or out of the pockets of others who were friends of the word of God.

It was a monumental task that this man undertook. And he did all the hard work, and took all the risks, and spent all the money for the sake of the *word* of God through the *prophets* of God! That is a lesson to us. Should we not also take great pains for the sake of God's word—both in feeding *ourselves*, spiritually, and in making sure that the word of God is available to *others*? By preserving the *physical* lives of these hundred men, Obadiah was enriching the *spiritual* lives of the thousands whom they would be able to teach once the storms of persecution blew over. By providing *physical* bread to these prophets, he enabled them to provide *spiritual* bread for who knows how many people.

We can be just as strategic, can't we? When you provide physical bread for a missionary family, how many hundreds of people are blessed with the bread of life through their work? The same is true when you give money to Bible societies, and inner-city outreaches, and Christian ministries of compassion, and so on. The effect of your few pounds or dollars, given to one ministry or missionary, is multiplied to untold hundreds and thousands. The same is true when you provide the physical bread that feeds your local pastor. In providing for his family's *physical* needs, you free him up to meet the *spiritual* needs of everyone in your congregation, and of many others who come to him for counselling, listen to his sermons online, or benefit when he preaches away from home.

There are surely other applications that could be made as well. But the simple principle is this: if we provide bread for just a few key 'prophets', we may actually be providing spiritual nourishment for thousands! And for each of us, just as for Obadiah, that is well worth the time, effort, money, and even risk it may involve.

So Obadiah's courage is a wonderful reminder of the value of the word of God. Finally, in the courage of Obadiah, we see a picture of …

### The love of the brethren

In many ways, we may find it hard to identify with Obadiah. He lived during an unusual period of persecution. He had an unusually high position in the government. And that position enabled him to help an unusually large number of the Lord's servants. So maybe we cannot relate to Obadiah in every aspect of his *circumstances*. But surely we ought to be able to find ourselves in rhythm with his *heart*. For it is the duty, instinct, and *privilege* of all God's children, just as it was for Obadiah, to love and care for our brothers and sisters in the Lord.

If you have done much travelling, perhaps you have seen the way Christians the world over seem to 'recognize' their brothers and sisters almost immediately—even if they have never met before. What a thrill it is to visit an unknown church on holiday, and to find yourself receiving dinner invitations from people you have never seen before, but who are family! What a joy to set out on a mission trip, and to find that Christians on the other side of the world are eager to welcome you 'home'!

In Christ, we are brothers and sisters! And thus, in Christ, we are there for one another—especially in times of need. That was the spirit of Obadiah, and that is the spirit of all God's children. We are family! We therefore have a God-given desire to help one another, to welcome one another, and to be there for one another—even if we have never met before.

If we are in Christ, we have all these desires within us by virtue of the new birth. But we must cultivate the desires, rather than assuming them. We must work to build lifestyles and schedules that will enable us to fulfil these God-given desires to welcome, love, and care for the brethren. Think about how you might do that, and especially so for *the persecuted* among us. For 1 Kings 18 is a story of the persecuted church. And meeting their needs was instinctive to Obadiah, just as providing bread, water, and prayer for the persecuted church ought to be normal, and even instinctive, for us as well. We ought to read a publication like the newsletter of The Voice of the Martyrs and think to ourselves: How can I provide these suffering brothers with 'bread and water'? What can I do to help those widows and orphans who have lost a husband and father because he dared to proclaim the gospel? How can I pray for their perseverance? That is simply the *Christian* way of thinking. But, again, that kind of thinking and feeling must be cultivated, and must find outlets for usefulness. I know of no better resource for cultivating a love for the persecuted church, and for finding outlets to serve them, than the free newsletter of The Voice of the Martyrs.[1]

The events of 1 Kings 18:4a are repeated all over the world today—and so, therefore, must be the events of verse 4b. That is to say that Satan always has his Jezebels ready to destroy the prophets, and other Christians too. But we have the privilege of being God's Obadiahs,[2] hiding them in caves and bringing them 'bread and water'—even, if necessary, at the risk of suffering with them.

Obadiah risked his neck for fellow believers. And we ought to be willing to do the same—not because we are imitators of Obadiah, mainly; but because we are imitators of Jesus. After all, did Jesus not say, 'Greater love has no one than this, that one lay down his life for his friends' (John 15:13)? And he said it, not mainly about us or Obadiah, but *about himself*! Jesus, like Obadiah, put his life on the line to rescue his friends from destruction. Indeed, he willingly *gave* his life for his friends. And the way in which he did so makes him ten thousand times greater than Obadiah. For Jesus did not give his life for us when we were out, like these prophets, proclaiming his word. No; Jesus laid down his life for us 'while we were yet sinners' (Rom. 5:8)! This is the greatest love of all!

Do you know this love of Christ? Do you know what it is to have your sins forgiven, your slate wiped clean, and your friendship with God restored—all because Jesus gave his life for you? If you do, the biblical implication is that, having experienced this kind of sacrificial love yourself, you will surely want to shower it upon other people as well. That is what the apostle John proclaimed in 1 John 3:16: 'We know love by this, that [Jesus] laid down His life for us; and we ought to lay down our lives for the brethren.'

That was what Obadiah was doing. Before he ever knew the Saviour's name, Obadiah was mirroring the love of Jesus.

So Obadiah is, in that sense, just another signpost on the Old Testament road that leads us to Christ. Obadiah's sacrificial love for God's people in 1 Kings 18 is a portrait of Christ. And, as we have been saying, Obadiah's sacrificial love for God's people is also a pattern for all those who follow Christ. So, for those of us who *do* know Jesus' name; for those of us who are far more aware of the work of Christ than Obadiah, from his Old Testament vantage point, could possibly have been— how much more ought *we* to bring 'bread and water' to God's people! How much more ought *we* to risk our lives on their behalf! How much more ought we to 'lay down our lives for the brethren'!

## Reflect on these points

1. *Think about Obadiah's courage once more—the way he feared the Lord more than the queen. Then ask yourself if there are situations in your life in which you have opportunity to show similar courage. Finally, pray that God would give you strength to do so.*

2. *In preserving the prophets, Obadiah also preserved the word of God for his countrymen. Ask God to show you some ways you might preserve and promote the word of God in your church, city, and nation—and even on the mission field.*

3. *Reflect on how Obadiah's courage (and potential self-sacrifice) mirrors that of Jesus. Thank God again that, in far greater ways than Obadiah, Jesus gave of himself to keep God's people alive. Reflect specifically on what Jesus has done for you.*

# Jehosheba:
## The faithful aunt

*When Athaliah the mother of Ahaziah saw that her son was dead, she rose and destroyed all the royal offspring. But Jehosheba, the daughter of King Joram, sister of Ahaziah, took Joash the son of Ahaziah and stole him from among the king's sons who were being put to death, and placed him and his nurse in the bedroom. So they hid him from Athaliah, and he was not put to death. So he was hidden with her in the house of the LORD six years, while Athaliah was reigning over the land.*

*(2 Kings 11:1–3)*

K ing Ahaziah was the last-surviving son of his father, Joram, King of Judah. His brothers before him, we are told in 2 Chronicles 22:1, had already been slain by a band of marauding Arabs. So, when Ahaziah himself died (2 Kings 11:1) in his twenties, all that was left of the royal lineage was a handful of little boys, sons of the now-deceased king. These few remaining heirs to the throne were still ambling around the palace holding their mother's hand and fighting with toy swords, not real ones.

These must have been startling and precarious days for this family who had been promised that their dynasty would last for ever (2 Sam. 7:16). The royal line, along with the promise, seemed to teeter on the brink of extinction. But in this sad turn of events, Ahaziah's idolatrous mother, Athaliah, saw a great opportunity. Instead of allowing the kingdom to pass to one of her grandsons, Athaliah would usurp the throne for herself. In order to do so, 'she rose and destroyed all the royal offspring'.

Athaliah slew her own grandsons so that she could be queen! She was a cruel, ruthless, coldblooded woman—which is no surprise, given that wicked Ahab was her father.

With this woman in the ascendancy, cruelty was the order of the day. All the young princes were marked out for slaughter. The royal line was about to be snuffed out completely and for ever. Yet a brave woman called Jehosheba, at the risk of her life, stepped into the fray, scooped up the boy-prince Joash, and kept him alive for six years, hidden in the temple of God.

As we read in verse 2, this Jehosheba was the sister of the recently deceased king (Ahaziah) and the daughter of his idolatrous father (Joram, the late husband of Athaliah). That would make Jehosheba the daughter (or perhaps step-daughter) of this ruthless, idolatrous queen mother. Yet, somehow, Jehosheba was a worshipper of the one true God, and not of the idols of her parents. We do not know exactly how Jehosheba, living in such a wicked family, came to trust in the Lord, but it is evident that she did. For, when she gathered up her nephew and went into hiding, her place of refuge was in 'the house of the LORD' (v. 3). Jehosheba took refuge in *God* and in his temple! She was a believer—and a brave one, at that!

It must have required tremendous courage for Jehosheba to have done what she did. It is surely difficult for any woman to stand up to an unbelieving mother, but Jehosheba's situation was infinitely more difficult. *Her* mother was a murderer—and of the cruellest kind. Athaliah was killing her own grandsons—Jehosheba's nephews! So surely, if Athaliah thought her daughter was standing in her way, she would have had no qualms about eliminating her as well. Yet, in spite of all these things, Jehosheba acted. She trusted in the Lord, and she acted!

Jehosheba could not save *all* the royal offspring. But she could perhaps at least rescue the baby—Joash, who was only about a year old when all this treachery took place. So we read in verses 2–3 that she sneaked into the place where the king's sons were being kept, awaiting execution, and that she stole her little nephew away and hid him (with the help of her husband, the priest—2 Chr. 22:11–12) for six years in the temple complex there in Jerusalem. I say that this was incredibly gutsy—and not just in the initial act of stealing Joash away. For six long years, Jehosheba walked to the market, attended family gatherings, worshipped at the temple, and went to bed at night ... never knowing if and when her secret might come out; never knowing if and when her head might be lopped off by Athaliah! Imagine living for 2,190 days constantly wondering if this day might be your last. That was the life Jehosheba chose for herself! And she is, therefore, another reminder of the great call for Christian courage: of the call to fear God more than we fear the queen, or the boss, or the government, or the unbelieving family member. As our own culture, like that of Athaliah's Judah, slips further and further into the abyss of idolatry, courage is the great need of the hour. What a portrait of it we have in this magnificent woman, Jehosheba!

We also have, in the example of Jehosheba, a powerful reminder concerning ...

## The glory of hidden service

By their very nature, Jehosheba's actions had to be hidden from public view—and for good reason! If what she had done began to be whispered in the streets of Jerusalem, it would soon be off with her head, and with the baby's, too! So we are not surprised that she kept her compassion and courage a secret for those six years. Boasting about these things, or being praised for them, would have been suicide.

Think about Jehosheba's secrecy, however, from a slightly different perspective. One nagging thought in the back of Jehosheba's mind for those seventy-two months was surely the concern of being found out and punished. But, if she was like most of us, another nagging thought may have been the fact that, as heroic as her actions had been, no one but her husband and the baby's nurse knew anything about them! Jehosheba could not bask in the glow of her accomplishments. She could not be patted on the back, praised, or spoken well of for her bravery. No one would have realized that a heroine was living in their midst. No one would even have known that she and her husband were spending the time, money, and energy it takes to raise a child from the age of one to the age of seven! So, if she was going to be courageous and faithful, mothering this child as her own, Jehosheba would have to do so in exchange for the applause of no one but God. She would have to do so looking to a long-term reward rather than any immediate gratification.

She would have to do so simply because it would render her faithful, and not because it would make her famous.

Perhaps it would be helpful for us, now and again, to ask ourselves if we are willing to have our lives and service to God play out in the same way as Jehosheba's. Though we will probably never be famous, we like at least to be recognized, do we not? We like people to say 'thank you' to us. We feel gratified when people take notice of how well we led the Bible study; or of how good we are with the children in the nursery; or of how seamlessly the fellowship meal went; or of how well we played that instrument. And, of course, we *ought* to recognize one another in these ways. This is part of the encouraging and building up that the New Testament urges us to do for one another.

But we must sometimes ask ourselves: How do I feel when nobody does that for *me*? How do I feel when my faithfulness, courage, or effort seems to go unnoticed? Perhaps even more key, we need to ask the question: Would I, like Jehosheba, do what I believe God is calling me to do even if I knew, *going into it*, that no one would know about it? Would you or I be willing to do what Jehosheba did—to risk our lives, or even just to put ourselves under financial and emotional strain for six long years—if we knew, ahead of time, that during all those many months our work would go unnoticed? Are we willing to perform service even when it is for God's eyes only?

There *is* a glory in serving in this obscure way! For did not Jesus teach us, in the Sermon on the Mount, that fruitful prayer is *secret* prayer; that faithful giving is *secret* giving; and that effective fasting is *secret* fasting? There is glory in hidden service, Jesus tells us. Why? Because, when you serve without any concern for the praise of other people, both you and God know that you really are serving *him*, and not just your own reputation. And, says Jesus on three consecutive occasions in Matthew 6, 'your Father who sees what is done in secret will reward you' (vv. 4, 6, 18).

How good it would be if we could learn, from Jehosheba, the glory of hidden service! We will do equally well if we can discern from her story ...

## The pattern of God's providence

Make no mistake: this is surely a story about the compassion and intervention of this courageous woman named Jehosheba. But, far more than that, it is a story about the compassion and intervention of her *God*! After all, Jehosheba (like us) could do nothing apart from the Lord. It was God who put her in the royal family in the first place, so that she might be in *a position* to save Joash's life. It was God who saved her out of the idolatry of her parents, so that she might have *the heart* to save Joash's life. And it was surely God who protected her from being found out when she *did* save Joash's life. Indeed, as we saw in verse 3, it was in God's own house that she and the baby found refuge!

So, more than anything else, this is a story of *God's* intervention! And it has a familiar ring to it, does it not? A baby boy who is destined to do great things for God; a monarch who feels threatened and wants the baby dead; and a courageous couple who take great risks in order to protect his little life. Where have you heard that story before? This account in 2 Kings 11 sounds strikingly similar to the story of young Moses in Exodus 1–2, does it not? It also sounds strikingly similar to Matthew 2, where Mary and Joseph have to take the baby Jesus into hiding to protect him from the bloodthirstiness and ambition of King Herod.

Why do I point out these similarities? Simply because there is a pattern in God's providence. We cannot always predict the *details* of how God is going to work things out, but God is not unpredictable. That is to say that God often works in patterns. We have just seen it in this pattern of baby boys, ruthless monarchs, and courageous couples. But there is an even broader pattern to notice in the stories of Moses, Joash, and Jesus—namely, that God often seems to allow his cause to hang quite precariously before he steps in and saves the day!

Is that not what we see here in 2 Kings 11, and in its parallels in the lives of Moses and Jesus? It seems, in each case, as if God allowed his good plans to come dangerously close to collapse. If, for instance, Joash had died, who would have been King of Judah? As we saw already, Joash's father, brothers, and all his uncles were dead. Athaliah's elimination of 'all the royal offspring' perhaps also meant that she eliminated not only Joash's brothers, but also any cousins who might have had a claim to the throne which she so desperately wanted for herself. So it would appear that Joash alone was left. Yes, it is possible that there was a third or fourth cousin, from somewhere back in the lineage, who could have been tracked down and brought to Jerusalem to be made king. But it seems improbable that this was the case. Athaliah's royal genocide seems to have been quite thorough. Indeed, Athaliah usurped the throne for six years, and during all those years no one appears to have stepped forward and claimed to have been a distant descendant of David.

The implication of 2 Kings 11 seems to be that, if Joash had been murdered, this royal dynasty that stretched all the way back to King David would have died with him. And, if that had happened, how could God have fulfilled his promise that David's dynasty would last for ever? God seems to have come dangerously near to allowing this cruel woman named Athaliah completely to wipe out his covenant with David!

How could God have let it get so close? How could he have allowed the situation to escalate to the point when 'all the royal offspring' were thought to be dead, and when the one living heir to David's throne was a one-year-old baby boy? In those pre-vaccination, pre-hospital, pre-modern-medicine days, babies surely died all the time. So how could God have cut it so close?

He could do so, for one thing, because he is absolutely sovereign! It did not matter what the statistics or the odds were. It did not matter what Athaliah planned to do. God knew he could and would keep Joash healthy and alive—and he did so! So we understand why God *could* cut it so close. But why *would* he? Why *would* he allow his promise and his kingdom to hover so near to extinction? Why did he not simply squash Athaliah like an ant under his heel? Why did he allow things to unravel to the place where such an amazing intervention was required in order to keep Joash, the kingdom, and the promises to David alive? And why did God do the same thing with Moses and with Jesus? In fact, why did God so often, in both the Old and New Testaments, seem to wait until things seemed almost irreversible and unredeemable before he stepped in and intervened?

Perhaps God allowed the situation in 2 Kings 11 (and so many others like it) to get to a place where things seemed almost totally hopeless so that we would know that it is he—not ourselves, our enemies, or our circumstances—that is in control of our lives and, indeed, of the course of world history. If God never allowed us to get to a place where all our planning failed, and all of the momentum seemed against us, and all human effort seemed like nothing more than spinning our wheels; if he allowed everything to go smoothly for us all the time, we might actually mistake the blessing of God for the fruits of our own wisdom, planning, and effort. We might actually begin to think that we were pretty smart and clever! But if, on the other hand, God did not intervene to pull us out of the quicksand at all, if he never interposed to snatch us from Athaliah's grip, we might begin to think that kings, queens, circumstances, and the winds of chance actually rule the day.

To put it more simply: in Bible history God often waited

until the last possible moment to intervene on behalf of his cause and his people so that they might know that their lives were in *his* hands, not their own; and so that they might learn that their *God*—not kings, rulers, and circumstances—rules in heaven and on earth!

In order that we might learn this lesson, these kinds of last-minute, impossible turnarounds become a pattern throughout the Bible. And, if they are a pattern throughout the Bible, we should not be surprised if God sometimes waits until all hope seems gone before he intervenes in *our* lives, as well! We should not be surprised if we find ourselves in places where we seem to be out of options; where all we have left to do is to cry out in desperate prayer. You may sometimes find yourself in exactly this position as it relates to some health or financial concern; or as a loved one lies seemingly unconscious on his or her deathbed, and still has not confessed Christ. You may think in these terms regarding the spiritual demise of Western culture, and our desperate need for revival. Many times, from a human perspective, all hope seems gone. But God specializes in intervening when hope seems to have run dry—so that we might know that it was *his* doing, not our own!

You may be reading these pages even now feeling as if *you yourself* are out of options. You may surmise that you have sinned your way past the point of no return, outlived your usefulness, or been dealt a blow from which you will never recover. But remember that, for six years, the people of Judah thought the royal line of David was extinct. For six years, while Joash was in hiding, the people must have thought that the dream was over; that their and their rulers' sins had taken them past the point of forgiveness, restoration, and a future. But God brought the royal dynasty back from what seemed like the dead, beginning in 2 Kings 11:4! And he can surely do the same for you, however far gone you may feel yourself to be. If you would only turn to this God, and to his Son, Jesus, you would be amazed at how he loves to intervene when it seems that all hope is gone!

Speaking of Jesus, we cannot read 2 Kings 11 without considering him. In 2 Samuel, as we have said, God promised David that his descendants would rule on a throne that would have no end. The rest of the Old Testament (for instance, Isaiah 11) makes it clear that this promise would ultimately be fulfilled in the coming of the Messiah himself. In other words, the Saviour of God's people—the one who would lay down his life for their sins; the one whose name we now know is Jesus—was going to come from the house of King David!

It was a wonderful promise—but it must not have seemed all that wonderful for the people living in the first three verses of 2 Kings 11. King Ahaziah's father and all his brothers had died before him. So every branch of the family tree of royal heirs seems to have been dead, except for King Ahaziah and his little boys. And when Ahaziah died, in 2 Kings 11:1, Athaliah 'rose and destroyed' all his sons as well (or so she thought).

Let us pause here to make sure we fully grasp what was at stake in 2 Kings 11. If God had not raised up Jehosheba to rescue one of those little boy-princes; and if God had not kept that boy-prince alive until he was ready to be king, and until he himself was capable of bearing royal offspring of his own—not only would God's promise *to David* have fallen to the ground unfulfilled, but also God's promise *to the world* could have fallen to the ground unfulfilled as well! Remember that the Saviour of the world was going to come through this very family—through the house and line of King David; through the sons, grandsons, and great-grandsons of this royal line. But if it had not been for Jehosheba, there would have been no more sons, grandsons, or great-grandsons! And if there had been no more sons, grandsons, and great-grandsons in the line of David, what would have become of baby Jesus?

Without 2 Kings 11:2, there may well have been no Luke 2! Without Jehosheba, there may well have been no Mary and Joseph, descendants of David, and no trip to Bethlehem to register for the census. Without God's intervention and Jehosheba's courage, there may well have been no manger, and no magi, and no baby born on that most holy night! And if there had been no baby Jesus, becoming flesh in the line of King David, there would have been no cross, no resurrection, no second coming, and no hope for us sinners! And if Jesus had remained in heaven, and never come as a human descendant of David, we would all be dead men and women walking!

We could go on and on, conjecturing about what might or might not have happened had little Joash perished here in 2 Kings 11. But the point is that God was *not* going to let those frightening possibilities come about! God had made a promise—not only to David, but to mankind! God *would* send a Saviour, who *would* be born into the family of David, and who *would* die for our sins! Nothing was going to stand in God's way. Herod could not derail God's plan in Matthew 2. Neither could Athaliah snuff it out in 2 Kings 11. God *would* send his Son as the heir of David the king. And that Son *would* 'save His people from their sins'!

So, how thankful should we be for God's work in the life of Jehosheba? Through her courage, God not only kept Joash alive, but he also kept the lifeblood of Jesus alive! And, in doing that, he kept all who belong to Jesus alive as well!

Reflect on these points

1. *Jehosheba's actions would have been courageous, praiseworthy, and exemplary even if the boy she rescued had not been the rightful king; and if her actions had taken place in Jersey rather than in Jerusalem! To be sure, the circumstances around this rescue operation made Jehosheba's actions all the more important. But rescuing a helpless child is significant and imperative, no matter what the circumstances may be. How might you be involved in such a mission—in rescuing the unborn, loving the abused, or redeeming children from the horrors of human trafficking?*

2. *Do you ever feel annoyed when no one notices your efforts and accomplishments? Are there any specific areas where you have been serving for the applause of*

*men rather than for the approval of God? Search your heart—and ask God to show you the glory of hidden service.*

3. *Think about some person or circumstance in your life that seems past the point of no return. How can the last-minute rescue of Joash give you hope? Spend some time meditating on God's providence in 2 Kings 11, asking him to grow your faith.*

# Ebed~melech:
## The compassionate foreigner

*Then they took Jeremiah and cast him into the cistern of Malchijah the king's son, which was in the court of the guardhouse; and they let Jeremiah down with ropes. Now in the cistern there was no water but only mud, and Jeremiah sank into the mud. But Ebed-melech the Ethiopian, a eunuch ... went out from the king's palace and spoke to the king, saying, 'My lord the king, these men have acted wickedly in all that they have done to Jeremiah the prophet whom they have cast into the cistern; and he will die right where he is because of the famine, for there is no more bread in the city.' Then the king commanded Ebed-melech the Ethiopian, saying, 'Take thirty men from here under your authority and bring up Jeremiah the prophet from the cistern before he dies.' So Ebed-melech took the men under his authority and went into the king's palace to a place beneath the storeroom and took from there worn-out clothes and worn-out rags and let them down by ropes into the cistern to Jeremiah. Then Ebed-melech the Ethiopian said to Jeremiah, 'Now put these worn-out clothes and rags under your armpits under the ropes'; and Jeremiah did so. So they pulled Jeremiah up with the ropes and lifted him out of the cistern, and Jeremiah stayed in the court of the guardhouse.*

*(Jer. 38:6–13)*

These were precarious times. Not far from Jerusalem were hordes of Babylonians, sent by God to chasten his people for years of sin. Defeat, destruction, and exile were imminent. Into this depressing milieu came the preaching of the prophet Jeremiah. He had been sent both to reprove the people of God for their sins and to instruct them in how they might wisely respond to the Lord's discipline. His reward for such faithful labours? With the king's approval (Jer. 38:5), 'they took Jeremiah and cast him into the cistern' (v. 6).

But into this bad situation stepped another of those Bible characters whose name we scarcely know, but whose life had major significance in the eyes of the all-seeing God. Ebed-melech, though he was Ethiopian, worked for the Jewish king. And Ebed-melech, as we read, stood *against* that king, and against the rising political tide of his day, in order that he might stand *with* the man of God, Jeremiah. To do so required the same kind of daring we have already witnessed in the lives of Obadiah and Jehosheba. It is not easy to stand against a sovereign who holds life and death in his hands! So, when we read of Ebed-melech, surely we admire *his courage*. But, in addition, we should also notice …

## His country

It is not without importance that Ebed-melech was Ethiopian. While it is possible that King Zedekiah had numbers of internationals working in his regime, the fact that Ebed-melech's nationality is mentioned three times (vv. 7, 10, 12) perhaps means that he was a bit of an oddity in the palace. He surely stood out as different—and even more so because it was he, the foreigner, who stepped in to protect God's prophet! Therefore Jeremiah was careful to record that this marvellous, courageous man was an 'Ethiopian', not an Israelite.

This drawing attention to the faithfulness of non-Israelites is actually a pattern throughout the pages of Scripture. It was a Samaritan (not an Israelite) who got down from his donkey to help a wounded traveller in Jesus' famous story in Luke 10. Similarly, when Jesus healed ten lepers in Luke 17, he was careful to point out that the only one who returned to give thanks was a 'foreigner'. We might also remember that it was a widow from the pagan land of Zarephath who exchanged kindnesses with the prophet Elijah (1 Kings 17). So Ebed-melech is simply part of a long line of non-Israelites who come in for commendation in Scripture. And there is a lesson in that—namely, that God is not constrained to redeem and make useful only those who have the proper religious upbringing. Indeed, God delights in adopting spiritual outsiders into his family!

Did Ebed-melech grow up pagan, and emigrate to the Promised Land only as an adult? Or had he grown up in Jerusalem, a son of immigrant (perhaps God-fearing) parents? We do not know for sure. But Jeremiah's consistent emphasis on his foreign nationality is a reminder that Ebed-melech, wherever he grew up, was still looked upon as an outsider. In spite of where he lived and worked as an adult, he was still an 'Ethiopian', not an Israelite. Indeed, as a foreigner (and especially as one who been emasculated), Ebed-melech likely enjoyed precious little access to the public worship in God's temple (see Deut. 23:1). He may rarely, if ever, have participated in the sacrifices and feasts which spoke of God's gracious forgiveness of sins. He probably had few of the advantages that normally bring people to faith. Yet we are told, in the last verse of Jeremiah 39, that in spite of all the disadvantages, Ebed-melech did indeed come to faith! The reason he helped Jeremiah was not just because he was a kindly fellow, but because he trusted the Lord.

Ebed-melech was an 'Ethiopian', not an Israelite. Yet here we find him, in the middle of the book of Jeremiah, a firm believer in the God of Israel. How did that happen? We do not know the details. But Ebed-melech is a wonderful reminder that, whatever the details, God loves to scoop up people who are 'far off' (Eph. 2:13) and bring them 'near'; that God's family is not merely open to a select few people who come from the right backgrounds and environments—but that the kingdom of God, the forgiveness of sins, and the prospect of usefulness in God's house are 'for all those who believe', as Paul puts it so succinctly in Romans 3.

Is this not wonderful news? Perhaps, like Ebed-melech, you grew up scarcely ever attending the public worship of God and knowing next to nothing about how your sins might be forgiven. You may have known precious little of the Bible, if anything at all. You were far off! Indeed, so were those of us who grew up in church every Lord's Day! For, even if we knew all the right answers from childhood, every Christian is fully aware of how often we rejected God's ways and lived for ourselves; of how often we turned our backs on Jesus and chose sin instead. None of us were born loving and trusting Jesus. Each one of us had to be born *again* in order to see and enter the kingdom of God (John 3). So, even if you grew up religious, there was a time when you were 'far off'. But I hope you can say that, whatever far country you came from (religious or not), God has brought you near!

We all ought to be able to see ourselves in Ebed-melech's reflection. If a staff photo had been taken in the palace at Jerusalem, people could have picked out Ebed-melech and said to themselves, 'Who is *that* fellow? He doesn't seem to belong, does he? What is *he* doing with the people of God?' If we are honest, we would say the same of ourselves if we saw a photo of the crowd at church on a Sunday morning. 'There I am with the people of God—singing his praises; holding his Word in my hand; serving his church. Perhaps I even have a leadership role. In some ways, it all seems so normal to me now. But when I consider the sinful country from which I came; when I consider how far off I once was—it seems almost preposterous that I should be in the photograph with the saints of God! And yet there I am, thanks to a God who calls those who are "far off" and brings them "near" by the blood of Christ.'

Ebed-melech is actually, therefore, a picture of every Christian. We are all spiritual foreigners who, by God's grace, have found our way into the family of God. Having experienced that grace, Ebed-melech was a changed man. As evidence of that fact, consider …

### His compassion

Yes, Ebed-melech was concerned about Jeremiah's fate simply because the king's henchmen were behaving 'wickedly' (v. 9). He acted, in other words, out of a concern for *righteousness*.

But what was just as amazing was how Ebed-melech acted out of a heart of *tenderness* as well.

Ebed-melech had to get Jeremiah out of that mud hole: that was the right thing to do. But he did not simply run as fast as he could to sling a rope down the mouth of the cistern and drag the prophet out! No, Ebed-melech actually had the foresight to stop off at the palace storerooms and grab some old worn-out T-shirts that Jeremiah might use to cushion the ropes and keep himself from rope burn! Isn't that tender, thoughtful, and compassionate?

We read this passage and say, 'Of course! Jeremiah was already weakened from lying in the mud. He probably already had terrific welts under his arms from the way Zedekiah's cronies had dangled him down the hole in the first place. So it made perfect sense for Ebed-melech to provide a little padding for Jeremiah to wrap around the ropes.' That is what we all think when we read this passage: Ebed-melech's actions were just common sense. But how many of us would have thought to stop at the storerooms and grab those old shirts? I might have been in such a hurry that Jeremiah's raw skin would not have occurred to me until I got him to the top and saw blood trickling down his arms! But it occurred to Ebed-melech. And, when we consider these events, we should marvel at—and imitate—this Ethiopian's resourcefulness, thoughtfulness, and compassion. All of God's people ought to think as Ebed-melech thought—to notice people in need, to long to help them, and then to get busy doing so. And all God's people ought to take thought, as Ebed-melech did, as to how to help most tenderly and compassionately.

Think about someone who is in the pit right now: someone you ought to go and help. Perhaps you are just the one to lend a hand! But as you prepare to go, ask yourself if there are any storerooms you should visit along the way; if there are any added touches of thoughtfulness and compassion you ought to add to your rescue ropes.

We ought all to be as ready to help—and as thoughtful in doing so—as this wonderful Ethiopian. And we ought to do this, let me add, not merely because we admire the example of Ebed-melech—but because Ebed-melech was following the example of the Lord! For is this not exactly how *God* treats *us*—with tender compassion?

Unlike Jeremiah, we often find ourselves in the mud because of our own foolishness and sin. And yes, sometimes God disciplines us painfully in order that we might get our feet back on firm ground. Sometimes, to teach us a lesson, he may well pull us up out of the pit with no padding at all! But very often, he 'pad[s] the ropes' (NIV). Very often, even when we deserve much rougher treatment, God draws us out of the pit gently— with his promises of forgiveness, the hope of reward for renewed obedience, and the kind words of Christian friends. Very often it is, as Paul said, God's 'kindness' that 'leads [us] to repentance' (Rom. 2:4).

Have you experienced this? Somehow or other, you found yourself in a miry pit. Perhaps it was your own fault you were down there. Perhaps, as for Jeremiah, it wasn't. But, in any case, there you sat. You would have been glad to be pulled out in any way possible—rope burns or no rope burns; pain or no pain. Indeed, if it was your own foolishness that got you into the pit, maybe you were expecting a good bit of discomfort on the way out. But you looked up and realized that God had not simply slung a rope down to you, but that, tied all up and down that rope, were various bits of precious cloth—Bible promises and encouragements—sent to ease your suffering!

That is the way God so often works—*wooing* us back to himself rather than *whipping* us into shape. The ultimate example of this is how he sent his Son. When God sent Jesus to rescue us from the mud of our sin, he did not send him with a rope to yank us up out of our mess. He did not send Jesus to save us roughly and forcefully. No, God sent Jesus binding up the broken-hearted, befriending the outcast, healing the sick, teaching the poor, and laying down his life as a payment for our sins! God sent Jesus to rescue us, not as a lion, but as a lamb—with an easy yoke and a light burden! And Ebed-melech is just another reminder that this is how God so often works. He 'pad[s] the ropes' (NIV). He shows tender compassion! And we ought to thank him doubly for it—and imitate him in it.

Finally, in addition to Ebed-melech's courage, country, and compassion, notice …

## His compensation

Given the size of the hordes *outside* the walls of Jerusalem, and given the madness of the king *inside* those walls, we should little wonder if we meet Ebed-melech in heaven someday and he tells us frankly, 'I thought I was done for!' It must have seemed to him that there was no way this storm could pass without the loss of his life. If Zedekiah didn't kill him for his loyalty to Jeremiah, Nebuchadnezzar, King of Babylon, would surely kill him for his loyalty to Zedekiah! So Ebed-melech must have considered himself as good as dead. And, from any human perspective, he was!

And yet, in Jeremiah 39, we read of a series of events that are (again, from a human perspective) completely unexpected:

> Now the word of the LORD had come to Jeremiah while he was confined in the court of the guardhouse, saying, 'Go and speak to Ebed-melech the Ethiopian, saying, "Thus says the LORD of hosts, the God of Israel, 'Behold, I am about to bring My words on this city for disaster and not for prosperity; and they will take place before you on that day. But I will deliver you on that day,' declares the LORD, 'and you will not be given into the hand of the men whom you dread. For I will certainly rescue you, and you will not fall by the sword; but you will have your own life as booty, because you have trusted in Me,' declares the LORD."'
>
> (Jer. 39:15–18)

The Babylonians were not averse to executing their captives. Many in Jerusalem perished when they finally broke through Jerusalem's walls. The king's own sons were slain before his eyes. But Ebed-melech, the palace official who was important enough to have had charge of thirty of the king's men (38:10), made it out alive! How? Did he find a really good hiding place? Or did Nebuchadnezzar's armies not suspect that an Ethiopian could have been such a high-ranking government official? We do not know the *secondary* answers to the question of Ebed-melech's astonishing escape from almost certain execution; but we do know the *primary* reason, from verses 17–18 above: God delivered him! That is to say that, if Ebed-melech found a place to hide, it was because the Lord provided it. Or if he slipped through the cracks because of his dark skin, it was because the Lord planned it that way. In other words, whatever the *other* reasons why Ebed-melech slipped through Nebuchadnezzar's clutches unscathed, the *main* reason was because God had promised he would!

But why had God made such a promise? We are told in verse 18 that Ebed-melech was given his life as 'booty'—as compensation, reward—for his having 'trusted' God. And this trust, of course, showed itself in the courage he demonstrated in rescuing Jeremiah! God rewarded Ebed-melech for his trusting faithfulness! And we can believe, on the authority of Scripture, that he will do the same for us. The Bible is replete both with promises and with examples like this of the fact that God 'is a rewarder of those who seek Him' (Heb. 11:6).

To be sure, we ought to show courage like Ebed-melech simply because it's right. And we ought to show compassion like Ebed-melech simply because it's good. We ought to serve the Lord and do good whether we are ever rewarded or not—

simply because God is worthy of our service and obedience.[1] But the reality is that God doesn't actually work things out that way. Yes, we *ought* to serve him without any regard to being compensated for our labours and faith. But the reality is that we never serve God without his taking notice. We never seek God without his being 'a rewarder of those who seek Him'. Our faith and obedience are *always* rewarded in some way or another.

Much of God's booty is stored up for us, not in this life, but in the next. So unlike Ebed-melech, we may not see immediate tangible rewards for our faith and obedience. But, if we seem to come up short here in this world, the reality is that heaven will be filled with the blessings of our trusting obedience!

God is 'a rewarder of those who seek Him'. So, if being courageous means you get yourself out on a limb for the Lord, you can rest easy knowing that he will not let you fall. If being compassionate towards others often seems a thankless job, keep at it! Even the person who gives away just 'a cup of water' for Jesus' sake 'will not lose his reward' (Mark 9:41). And surely neither will you!

Most of all, trust God! Ebed-melech was able to do what was right, come what might, because he trusted that God would take care of him, whether in the short term or the long—and he was not let down. For God has never yet allowed those who trust in him to be disappointed!

*Reflect on these points* ➤

Reflect on these points

1. *Can you remember what it was like when you, like Ebed-melech, were a 'foreigner'—when you were far from God? Think back to those days—not to wallow in old guilt, but to gain perspective on all God has done in you. What changes have you seen, by his grace? Pause and thank God for them!*

2. *Do you know anyone who is in a kind of cistern? How might you help that person out? And, as you run to do so, are there any thoughtful gestures or 'pieces of padding' you might bring along?*

3. *Dwell for a moment or two on the rewards laid up for God's people in heaven. Then think on some area where you are tempted to give up serving God or others because it seems so thankless. Is it thankless, really, in light of 'the glory that is to be revealed to us' (Rom. 8:18)?*

# John Mark:

## A runaway restored

*After some days Paul said to Barnabas, 'Let us return and visit the brethren in every city in which we proclaimed the word of the Lord, and see how they are.' Barnabas wanted to take John, called Mark, along with them also. But Paul kept insisting that they should not take him along who had deserted them in Pamphylia and had not gone with them to the work. And there occurred such a sharp disagreement that they separated from one another, and Barnabas took Mark with him and sailed away to Cyprus. But Paul chose Silas and left, being committed by the brethren to the grace of the Lord. And he was traveling through Syria and Cilicia, strengthening the churches.*

*(Acts 15:36–41)*

Mark's missionary story actually had a good beginning. A little while after Jesus' death, resurrection, and ascension, Peter, the great apostle, had been imprisoned for preaching Christ. But, with the help of an angel, he miraculously escaped in the middle of the night and went straight to a house where many of his fellow believers were still awake, holding a prayer meeting. One of the most memorable things about that night was that the girl who came to the door when Peter knocked was so excited to run and tell the others that he was alive that she forgot to open the door and let Peter in! Perhaps less remembered is the fact that the house where the prayer meeting took place belonged to a woman called Mary (Acts 12:12), 'the mother of John who was also called Mark'.

Mary's son John Mark was evidently a devout and gifted

man. For the apostle Paul had been visiting Jerusalem around the time of Peter's miraculous deliverance, and, when he and his partner Barnabas went back to Antioch to resume ministering in the church there, they took John Mark along with them (Acts 12:25)—probably because they saw in him the potential to be a useful partner in ministry.

Some time after their return, the thriving church in Antioch made one of the best decisions any church ever made—they sent Paul and Barnabas away as missionaries (Acts 13:1–3), carrying the good news of Jesus around the north-eastern Mediterranean basin. And, as we may surmise from the last few verses of Acts 15, they took Mark with them.

John Mark had been sent out as a missionary assistant to two of the greatest men in the early church. But something embarrassing and painful happened on that momentous journey. When they reached a place called Pamphylia, John Mark, for reasons we are not told, 'left them and returned to Jerusalem' (Acts 13:13). This desertion was surely hard for the two older men to swallow, and must have made for some awkward moments when Paul and Barnabas eventually arrived back in Antioch. So awkward were the relationships, in fact, that when it was time for the team to set out on a second missionary journey, there was 'a sharp disagreement' between the two great missionaries (15:39). Barnabas thought Mark should be given another chance, and wanted to restore him to the missionary team. Paul would not hear of it. So the two leading missionaries of the day parted ways. Barnabas took

Mark and went south-west, and Paul took a new partner, Silas, and headed north-west. What a sad piece of church history Acts 15 details—with Mark right at the centre.

Often (and tragically), when such a split occurs between brothers in Christ, there is never any restoration. In fact, so strong were the feelings in this instance that we might assume that the same would have been said of Paul, Barnabas, and Mark. But, if we read the rest of the New Testament carefully, we discover that Mark's name appears several more times—often in happy connection with Paul's—providing a joyful outcome to this very public division.

Several years after this painful dispute, Paul found himself imprisoned for the gospel's sake—probably in the vast metropolis of Rome. During that imprisonment, he wrote letters to some of the believers with whom his heart and prayers were so lovingly entangled. And in two of those letters, he mentioned that John Mark was there with him during his hour of trial (see Col. 4:10–11 and Philem. 24)! We are not certain whether Mark had actually been imprisoned with Paul, or whether he was simply living in Rome, paying Paul visits, and encouraging his spirits during the apostle's stay in prison. But, one way or another, the once-broken relationship was restored! We are not told how or when, but it is very clear that the two men were of one heart once more. So much so that, a few years later, when Paul was once again in prison for Jesus' sake (and realizing that he would probably not make it out alive), he asked Timothy to bring

*Mark* to him in prison (2 Tim. 4:11), 'for', said Paul, 'he is useful to me for service'.

What an amazing turnaround! Add in the fact that Mark, after his reconciliation with Paul, was also a co-worker of Peter's (1 Peter 5:13); and that, in addition to all this later travelling and ministering with the apostles, he wrote one of the four Gospels—and we have a beautiful picture of a man who had once fallen hard and failed miserably, but who became quite useful to the Lord and his people over the long haul of his life! Indeed, Barnabas's willingness to take him along so soon after he fell may be evidence that Mark's restoration happened even sooner than the apostle Paul was willing to recognize!

'John who was also called Mark' is, I think you will agree, an interesting case study. He is well worth a little observation—both for those of us who have failed miserably a time or two ourselves, and for those of us who are well aware how easily such a fall could happen to any Christian anywhere. So, as we follow Mark over the course of his life and ministry, let's make two primary observations from the life of this restored runaway. The first is simply this:

### The frailty of Christian disciples

Mark's missionary story is memorable for all the wrong reasons. Indeed, his failure is probably more memorable to a casual reader of the New Testament than is his restoration. Yes, Barnabas was willing, quite early on, to restore him to service (Acts 15:37), but we are told nothing of their missionary work together. And, while we do discover, as we read on in the New

Testament, that Mark and Paul were eventually reconciled and were once again able to partner in the Lord's work, we learn this only through a few hints placed here and there in Paul's epistles—hints that the casual Bible reader might easily overlook. And so, were it not for the Gospel he wrote, many Christians might scarcely remember Mark as anything other than a runaway disciple. And, while he was far more than that, Mark's running out on the Lord's work is recorded in Scripture for a reason, and bears some consideration on our part.

Our goal is not to beat Mark up for his failure and desertion, but simply to allow his example to make us a little more realistic about what Christian disciples are really like. For, if there is anything that Mark's failure teaches us, it is that even the best Christians are much more fragile, weak, and prone to give up than we would probably like to believe. Remember that Mark was a man of obvious gifts. He wrote one of the four Gospels! And he showed enough promise to have been invited along on one of the most important missionary journeys ever undertaken! So Mark was no casual Christian. He was a man of real solidity and potential. And yet even he called it quits at one point. Even someone this promising backpedalled—not necessarily on being a Christian, but on the work that God had called him to do.

So I simply say that Mark is a reminder to us. We are *all* similarly frail. How many of us have been tempted, at one point or other, to just give up? To stop serving the Lord? To give in to some sinful pattern? We are so weak, changeable, and frail.

Of course, our frailty is not an *excuse* if we should desert the Lord or his work. But we should not be surprised if, from time to time, we find ourselves—or our brothers and sisters—struggling to 'run with endurance the race that is set before us'. The struggle is not necessarily a sign that we are not real Christians; nor is it necessarily a sign that we will never be useful again. It is simply proof that we, like Mark, are far more spiritually fragile than we tend to realize in those moments when all is going well.

We are all so feeble and faint-hearted! It does not matter if we are as gifted as Mark was, or come from the same kind of committed Christian family. We are weak, breakable, frail human beings who need God, as we sometimes sing, 'every hour'![1]

Indeed, we need the Lord every *moment* of the day. And we need *his gospel* every moment, too! That is what Mark's struggles teach us. We are sinners, and we need the blood of Christ and the forgiveness of sins every moment. We need, every moment, the promise that he will never leave us or forsake us. And, after some of our darkest moments, we need someone like Barnabas to come along and give us a second chance to be useful to the Lord.

So one main reminder we garner from the life of 'John who was also called Mark' is, very simply, the frailty of Christian disciples—all of them! But, on the other side of the coin, Mark's story teaches us …

## The beauty of Christian restoration

Mark's restoration is the real marrow of his story—the factor that makes him so worthy of our consideration. Even though Mark tucked tail and ran out on God's work, he came back to the Lord. He came back to his friends Barnabas and Paul, and was restored! But my aim, in this heading, is not simply to show *that* Mark was restored, but rather to show how glorious and *beautiful* his restoration was! Keep that aim in mind as you read on.

Note well that Mark's desertion (Acts 13) and the division it fostered (Acts 15) were recorded many years after the fact, and by a man (Luke, the author of Acts) who knew how well the situation had turned out. Luke, as a friend of and fellow worker with both Paul and Mark (Philem. 24), knew that God had got Mark back on track, and back in communion with Paul. So Luke could have just smoothed this whole incident over as he wrote Acts 13 and 15, saving his friends Paul and Mark some embarrassment in the process. He could have simply informed his readers in Acts 15 that Paul and Barnabas went their separate ways, without telling us how acrimonious the split really was, or that Mark was the reason for it. But Luke did not write that way. He did not sugarcoat these sad events. Instead, he was startlingly forthright about how badly Mark behaved. He made it clear that Mark's departure was a hard blow to Paul and Barnabas.

Why did Luke do this? Why was he so blunt about the failings of his friends and gospel companions? Or perhaps it is better to ask: Why would *the Holy Spirit* have inspired Luke to write in this way? Surely in order to show us how fragile Christians really are, as we said above. But I wonder if the Holy Spirit did not also have another purpose in mind as he inspired Luke to record Mark's desertion and its fallout. Perhaps the Holy Spirit drove Luke's quill along to record Mark's failure in the annals of Scripture, not so much in order to make Mark look *bad*, but to make his restoration look as *amazing* as it actually was! To borrow another preacher's illustration, perhaps the Spirit's intent was to record the black marks on Mark's record as something like the black cloth laid down by a jeweller beneath the sparkling items in his display case. The black background enables us to see the brilliance of his diamonds all the more clearly![2] And we certainly see the beauty of Mark's later faithfulness all the more vividly when we set it against the black backdrop of his early failure.

That is what the Holy Spirit, I believe, was doing in recording Mark's desertion in Pamphylia. He did not shrink from telling Mark's failure as it truly was—not in order to stain Mark's reputation, but so that his readers might be all the more amazed to see Mark's name, at a later date, written in glowing terms at the end of Paul's epistles—and in full capital letters at the top of one of the four Gospels!

The book of Acts makes much of Mark's failures because the depth of his sin actually serves to make Mark's restoration all the more amazing and, indeed, surprising! That's right: Mark's turnaround is almost as surprising as it is beautiful. Indeed, maybe it is so wonderful to read what became of Mark just because it is not at all what we might have anticipated!

Think it out: if all you had ever read about Mark was that he'd deserted his missionary partners in Acts 13—if you had no idea that this was the same Mark who wrote the Gospel, or that Paul spoke so well of him later in the New Testament, or that Barnabas was so ready to forgive and partner with him once more—what might you conclude about 'John who was also called Mark'? Perhaps you would read Luke's dark report and write Mark off altogether. 'Well, that's the way it goes. Some people fade in and out of the church. Others keep going. I suppose that's the end of Mark. Now let's go on and see what happened with Paul and Barnabas and the others.' That is what we might be prone to do when we read that 'John [Mark] left them and returned to Jerusalem'. Surely that is what many Christians who *lived through* the events of Acts 13 could have done! How easy it would have been for them simply to assume that this was the end of Mark's usefulness; or to just move on from this episode, trying to forget it ever happened; or even to hold a grudge. Even Paul seems to have struggled not to file Mark away in the category of 'useless'!

It is easy to forget those who walk away from God's work, is it not? Or, if we do not forget them, it is easy to hold out very little hope that they will ever again be what they once were. We may *wish* otherwise; but do we really *expect* to witness a glorious restoration? Do we watch for it, as the prodigal's father watched the horizon, anticipating his son's return home? Do we pursue it, as Barnabas pursued the reinstatement of young Mark?

In the secular world, such forgiveness and restoration may be rare indeed. But in the world of the church of Jesus Christ, it really *should* be a normal thing to see people who have let others down and severely damaged their testimony actually being restored to fellowship and usefulness! When it happens, we are often surprised; but we shouldn't be, given the forgiving heart of our God!

Isn't the whole Bible one long running account of people who really made a mess of things, but were restored to faith and faithfulness? That is the message of the gospel—that God sent his Son into the world to save, not the righteous, but sinners; to be the great physician, not for the spiritually healthy, but for the sick! The Bible's good news is that Jesus is willing to leave the ninety-nine sheep out in the countryside to go in search of the one that has strayed! That is the gospel! And that is the pattern, so often, in the Scriptures! So it really should not surprise us to see the paradigm repeated in the story of Mark, or in the lives of Marks all around us today. In fact, it should not surprise us to see the paradigm repeated in our own lives—to see ourselves stumble badly in our walk of faith; but then to feel the Lord's kind and nail-printed hands picking us up, dusting us off, and lifting our chins once more!

Perhaps even now, though you sit with a Christian book in

your hand, you feel your life has been a slow drift away from God. Or maybe you can pinpoint a time, in recent weeks or months, when, like Mark, you just quit. Maybe you didn't quit on Christianity altogether, but you quit believing some promise; or praying for some need; or reading your Bible; or doing for God what you used to do; or fighting that besetting sin.

Does any of this sound familiar? Have you quit? I do not want for a moment to minimize the seriousness of your drifting or quitting. But I do want to remind you that you are no different from Mark. He was a missionary—but he got up one day and walked out on his calling, leaving his friends in a jam in the process! Perhaps, even to him, it seemed as if his days of usefulness were over. Perhaps he thought he would never really be happy in the Lord again. But look at him by the time we reach the end of the New Testament: he has gone back to the mission field, thanks to the patience and mercy of his cousin Barnabas. He has written his Gospel, to be read by millions for multiplied centuries ever since. And he has been restored to friendship with Paul, and even been requested by the apostle to come and help him die well!

In Acts 13:13 Mark is one of the most disappointing characters in the New Testament. But, by the end of the New Testament's chronicles, his is one of the greatest redemption stories in the whole Bible! And the same sort of turnaround could happen in you or me, no matter how hard we have stumbled. That is why Jesus came and died—so that we might be surprised by how willing he is to take us back, even when we have gone over a cliff, spiritually. So let us, like 'John who was also called Mark', run to him and be restored!

## Reflect on these points

1. *Think back on Mark's frailty. Do you believe that you are just as prone to stumbling as he was? What are some areas of personal vulnerability you might shore up with prayer and accountability?*

2. *Mark's restoration was as surprising as it was wonderful! Is there anyone in your Christian circle who has fallen away or stumbled badly? Have you written him or her off? Or are you hopeful that, if Mark could return to usefulness, so might your friend? Pray for that person now.*

3. *Think about a time in your life when you witnessed a restoration like that of Mark. Maybe it was your own, or that of someone in your church or family. Marvel afresh at God's goodness—and thank him once more!*

# Priscilla and Aquila:
## Paul's right-hand man
### ... and woman!

*After these things [Paul] left Athens and went to Corinth. And he found a Jew named Aquila, a native of Pontus, having recently come from Italy with his wife Priscilla, because Claudius had commanded all the Jews to leave Rome. He came to them, and because he was of the same trade, he stayed with them and they were working, for by trade they were tent-makers. And he was reasoning in the synagogue every Sabbath and trying to persuade Jews and Greeks ... Paul, having remained many days longer, took leave of the brethren and put out to sea for Syria, and with him were Priscilla and Aquila. In Cenchrea he had his hair cut, for he was keeping a vow. They came to Ephesus, and he left them there.*

*(Acts 18:1–4, 18–19)*

Priscilla and Aquila's names are sprinkled throughout the New Testament—three times in Acts 18, and three times in Paul's letters. As we read above, this couple moved from the great metropolis of Rome to the bustling city of Corinth during a time of persecution against the Jews (around AD 49[1]). Having come to Corinth, they came into a friendship with the apostle Paul (who was also new to the city), and the three of them set up shop together, making tents.

Paul, however, had not come to Corinth primarily to engage in business, but to preach the gospel. This he did, remaining in Corinth for some time and preaching first in the synagogue and later in a private house. Many people came to faith, and a church was born. But eventually the time came for Paul to move on and preach elsewhere. So he set out for Syria, spent time in a city called Cenchrea, and also preached briefly in Ephesus, the grand city of Asia Minor (in modern-day Turkey). And who was with him on these gospel journeys? According to Acts 18:18, Priscilla and Aquila had joined the missionary team!

We must therefore surmise that, somewhere along the way, these two Jewish tent-makers had been converted to Christ. Priscilla and Aquila had believed the message Paul preached, so much so that they were now willing to help him promote it around the Mediterranean world. Perhaps they had heard the gospel in their native Pontus and become believers before ever meeting Paul. Or perhaps they came to Christ during those eighteen months of working beside him in Corinth, hearing informal sermons as they sat across the table from the apostle, sewing and patching tents together day by day. Or maybe they were converted through the public meetings at which Paul preached on the Sabbaths in that city.

However it happened, Priscilla and Aquila were now disciples of Jesus. Indeed, they were committed enough to uproot themselves from their new home in order to travel with (and perhaps assist) Paul on his missionary tours. So the trio landed together in Ephesus towards the end of Paul's second missionary journey. And, when it came time for Paul to move on from his brief stay in the city, he left Priscilla and Aquila there, as we read in Acts 18:19—probably to keep up a gospel testimony after he had gone. Evidently Paul realized that, if his friends remained in Ephesus, they would be valuable leaders in furthering the gospel work which he had briefly begun in that city. And valuable leaders they proved to be! For, when an eloquent preacher came to town, they were biblically astute enough to notice that his theology was not quite fully developed, and to pull him aside and set him on a straighter course:

> Now a Jew named Apollos, an Alexandrian by birth, an eloquent man, came to Ephesus; and he was mighty in the Scriptures. This man had been instructed in the way of the Lord; and being fervent in spirit, he was speaking and teaching accurately the things concerning Jesus, being acquainted only with the baptism of John; and he began to speak out boldly in the synagogue. But when Priscilla and Aquila heard him, they took him aside and explained to him the way of God more accurately.
>
> (Acts 18:24–26)

When we pass out of Acts 18 and on to the rest of the New Testament, we discover that this faithful couple stayed on with the church in Ephesus where Paul had left them in the early 50s AD. For, when Paul returned to Ephesus some time later, he wrote a letter from that city to the congregation he had planted in Corinth, in which he passed along greetings from Priscilla and Aquila (1 Cor. 16:19). So they were evidently still serving in the church in Ephesus when Paul wrote 1 Corinthians in the mid-50s. According to 2 Timothy 4:19, they seem also to have been with Timothy, who was perhaps also in Ephesus[2] when Paul wrote that letter in the mid-60s. So they had a long history with the Ephesian congregation, and were no doubt a great blessing to it! In between the two letters mentioned above, however, Paul wrote his famous letter to the church at Rome. And, near the end of that letter (16:3–5), Paul dropped a personal note to his friends Priscilla and Aquila. So they had apparently gone back to live in the empire's capital, at least for a season![3]

Let us summarize: when we bring all the different biblical threads together, we discover that Priscilla and Aquila were a devout Christian couple and a huge asset to gospel ministry over the course of many years. Evidently, during the span of a decade and a half, they moved from Rome, to Corinth, to Ephesus, back to Rome, and then possibly back to Ephesus again—serving the churches and keeping in touch with their beloved apostle all along the way! No wonder William Hendriksen called them 'great travelers'![4] They were great Christians, too!

Priscilla and Aquila were two significant and important people in the New Testament period. They were key members of several of the most important churches in the world at that time. Even more impressively, Paul tells us in Romans 16:4 that 'all the churches of the Gentiles' knew their reputations and thanked God for them! Yet, because we have to turn back and forth from Acts to Romans, to 1 Corinthians, to 2 Timothy, pulling together a verse here and a verse there in order to piece together their history, Priscilla and Aquila are not as well known today as perhaps they should be.

I am convinced, however, that if we knew these two better,

we would be amazed at their faith, and spurred on to imitate it. So let's unpack their story in a little more depth, drawing four lessons from it. First of all, from what we have seen already, we are reminded of …

## The value of gospel partnerships

We may sometimes picture the apostle Paul travelling the known world like a folk-hero, single-handedly preaching the gospel and planting churches, strong as thunder. But that is far from an accurate picture. The truth is that Paul understood that he was no lone ranger—as evidenced by the fact that he was always looking for and enlisting helpers! Indeed, some of his letters close like movie credits, with a list of people who made his ministry possible. And when we gather together all those thank-you lists, we discover that (with only two or three possible exceptions) no one seems to have been as valuable to Paul's work as Priscilla and Aquila were!

The fact that Paul mentions this husband–wife team in three different letters, spread out over roughly a decade in their writing, surely demonstrates how much they meant to him—both when they were together and when they were apart. In Corinth, they opened their home to him (Acts 18:3). He had left them in Ephesus because he could trust them to minister the gospel there. No doubt they always prayed for his work, even when they did not know where his travels might have taken him. Perhaps they even supported him financially. Even more significantly, Paul wrote in Romans 16:4 that there was even a time when they 'risked their own necks' on his behalf! There were few people who could be counted upon like Priscilla and Aquila. And happy is the pastor or missionary who has a few people like this in his church or on his mailing list!

Priscilla and Aquila are a bright example of how important it is that Christians partner together in the work of the gospel. If *Paul* needed help, how much more do *our* pastors, teachers, deacons, elders, missionaries, and so on? Ministers and Christian leaders are far more fragile than they might appear when they stand before the congregation on a Sunday morning. They need their own Priscillas and Aquilas much more than perhaps those helpers realize.

Not everyone will preach the gospel or start churches like Paul. But for every Paul, there must be dozens of Priscillas and Aquilas who teach classes, disciple new believers, help with practical matters, provide lodging, open their homes for church gatherings (Rom. 16:5; 1 Cor. 16:19), offer leadership, pray for the work, support financially, and so on. So we must all find our own places in gospel partnership. We must all find our own gifts and roles in the church—and fulfil them with all the zeal of this faithful Jewish couple!

Priscilla and Aquila remind us of the value of gospel partnerships. But, secondly, we can also learn from them ...

### The significance of Christian women

Have you noticed how I keep referring to this couple with the wife's name first? I have consistently called them *Priscilla* and Aquila, not *Aquila* and Priscilla. The reason for that is simply because that is the way the biblical authors refer to them four out of the six times they are mentioned in the Scriptures. Both Paul and Luke (the author of Acts) usually mention Priscilla's name first. And that should strike us as odd. For, even in our twenty-first-century culture, we still usually refer to couples as Jim and Nancy, not Nancy and Jim. Indeed, the fact that women typically take their husband's last name is a reflection of this same sense of order—an order that was perhaps even more pronounced in the ancient world.

But here we have both Paul and Luke mentioning Priscilla first most of the time. Why? It is possible that she was an even more looked-up-to Christian than her husband. Her reputation in the churches may have carried even greater weight than did his! So much so that, when Paul thought of his wonderful friends and gospel partners, he often thought of Priscilla first!

This is the same apostle who wrote that he did 'not allow a woman to teach or exercise authority over a man' (1 Tim. 2:12), and who prescribed that ministers and elders should, without exception, be male (1 Tim. 3:2).[5] His high opinion of Priscilla by no means overturns those instructions. Yet it is worth noting that, although Paul would never have thought of appointing Priscilla as an elder in the church, he *did* recognize her high level of Christian competence and service. Paul did not, as some would have us believe, have a problem with women! Rather, he always found them to be very helpful and firm partners in the faith. And he always found ways of commending them for it.

So let us surely recognize the distinction in male and female roles—both in the home and in the church. Let us honour what the Bible teaches about submission and headship, and masculinity and femininity. But let us also recognize that women are far more important to the church than some Christian men may want to realize! Indeed, there is not a church I know of that could survive without its Priscillas! So women should be honoured in our churches, and should be encouraged and allowed to rise to Priscilla-like levels of value to the kingdom of God.

Now, thirdly, from the example of Priscilla and Aquila, let us thank God for …

### The blessing of biblical correction

Is it really a blessing to receive correction? The eloquent preacher Apollos would tell us that it is! Do you remember his story from the last few verses of Acts 18? While Priscilla and Aquila were living in Ephesus, Apollos arrived in that city and began to preach. In many ways, his preaching was fantastic! He was 'an eloquent man' we are told in verse 24, and a great student of the Bible as well. According to verse 25, Apollos seems to have rightly understood the person and work of the Saviour and was fervent to preach them. But we are told at the end of that verse that there was a problem. Apollos was not yet fully informed theologically. Though he was 'mighty in the Scriptures' and accurately understood the facts about Jesus, this eloquent preacher was 'acquainted only with the baptism of John'.

It is difficult to nail down exactly what this means. Since our focus in these pages is on Priscilla and Aquila, and not directly on Apollos, we will not take time to trace out the details. Let it suffice to say that, for all that he had right, something was still amiss in his teaching.

What were Priscilla and Aquila to do, sitting in the congregation listening to this man's powerful but clearly deficient preaching? Not only were they theologically astute enough to notice his mistakes, but they were also courageous enough (v. 26) to point them out to him! Beyond that, these two evidently pulled Apollos aside and corrected his vision in such a wise and gentle way that, far from giving up the ministry in shame and discouragement, he actually came to see 'the way of God more accurately', and went on preaching with far greater effectiveness than ever before (vv. 27–28)!

Don't we all need this kind of correction from time to time? Don't we all need someone to come along, now and again, and help us clean off our theological glasses? We all have blind spots; we all, on occasion, need correction. Sometimes we need it in the realm of our theology. Just as often, for many of us, we need it in the realm of our lifestyle and behaviour. And praise God if he should send us a Priscilla or an Aquila to show us 'the way of God more accurately'! For me their names were not Priscilla and Aquila, but Scott and Heather. The value of the redirection they offered me during my seminary days has proven incalculable. Perhaps even now you too can see in your mind's eye someone who was exactly this kind of help to you at some point along your spiritual journey; someone who showed you 'the way of God more accurately'.

We all need Priscillas and Aquilas in our lives. And thus we should all, like Apollos, open our ears to them when they come along. Just as importantly, some of us also need to be willing to *be* Priscillas and Aquilas for our brothers and sisters in Christ—to gently pull a misled or immature Christian aside and help him or her see things a little more clearly. That is the blessing of biblical correction!

Finally, let us allow the lives of Priscilla and Aquila to help us marvel at ...

## The mystery of God's providence

Do you remember how Paul got connected with this fascinating couple in the first place? It was not because he put out this 'Help Wanted' advertisement in the *Corinthian Times*:

> Energetic and courageous Christian couple required for assistance in missionary work and church-planting. Theological acumen a necessity. Must be willing to travel. Spare bedroom and tent-making skills a plus.

That was not how Paul, Priscilla, and Aquila were brought together in this strategic friendship! It was not *their* manoeuvring or planning that brought them together. Indeed, when they first met, I am sure these three had no inkling of all that they would accomplish together. Paul was simply looking for a friendly place to stay in a new city, and a little income on the side (18:3). Priscilla and Aquila were also new to the city (having been run out of Rome by the emperor, v. 2), and were perhaps in need of some help getting their fledgling business off the ground. And, because they were all tent-makers, a match was made!

The story is really quite remarkable. Paul needed gospel partnerships. And, in Corinth, he found one of the greatest sets of friends that any preacher or missionary ever had! But he found them, not as a result of his own ingenuity or foresight, but because a cruel pagan king hundreds of miles away issued a despotic decree; and because an unknown Jewish couple had to leave the imperial capital; and because they just 'happened' to arrive in Corinth at around the same time as the apostle Paul; and because they all just 'happened' to possess the same trade skills!

The first three verses of Acts 18 present an incredibly unlikely chain of events that brought Paul, Priscilla, and Aquila together—one that not even the most clever and devout Christian could have dreamed up, much less engineered. But God brought it together without Paul, Priscilla, or Aquila having a clue of the good he was doing for them behind the scenes. *God* made this gospel partnership come together. *God* put Priscilla and Aquila in the right place at the right time to show hospitality to Paul. *God* brought Priscilla under the preaching and influence of Paul so that she might become the woman of excellence that she became. And *God* brought Priscilla and Aquila to Ephesus at just the right time to be of service to a promising preacher in need of direction. So *God* must receive the praise!

In the early 60s AD, Paul wrote his famous letter to the church at Ephesus—the church that, at least at one point, met in Priscilla and Aquila's house (1 Cor. 16:19). Though we do not know for sure where he and his wife were living at that point, it is quite possible that Aquila was in the crowd that Sunday as Paul's letter was read for the first time in the Ephesian church. If he was, what thoughts might have run through his mind as the reader came to the middle of the second chapter and passed on Paul's reminder that any good work we ever do is a work 'prepared beforehand' by God himself? Aquila, of all people, could vouch for the truth of Ephesians 2:10. And I wonder if he might have stood and spoken to the gathered crowd along these lines:

> Oh yes, brothers and sisters, what Paul says is true. All our good works truly have been 'prepared beforehand' by a mighty and sovereign God. A dozen years or so ago Priscilla and I left Rome in shame and discouragement. The emperor threw us out of our home. It was a terrible time. We honestly wondered why God was doing this to us. But then we got to Corinth and met Paul. We heard the glorious gospel of Jesus week after week after week—in the church, and all day long at work! And we began to have our hearts warmed and our minds shaped and instructed. Eventually, we were able to help Paul with some discipling here and there. And now

look at us! We have a whole church gathered here on our living-room floor! But none of it would ever have happened, brothers, if God had not allowed Claudius to throw us out of our home! None of it would have happened if God had not brought us to Corinth just in time to meet Paul. None of it would have happened if we had been trained in sheep-herding rather than in tent-making!

Brothers and sisters, you must understand that we did not set out with some great agenda for how we were going to be useful to God. And, even if we had done, we would never have planned it *this* way! But you see, God worked it all out just right! So never doubt that what Paul is saying here is true, brothers and sisters of the Ephesian church. God has plans for you! He sent his Son to die for your sins, and to give you new life by his resurrection from the dead. And he has work already 'prepared' for you to do with that new life. But it is, and always will be, *his* work! For, as Paul says, all of us—Priscilla, me, and each one of us—'are *His* workmanship'. Our circumstances have fallen out just as *he* has ordained. Our lots have fallen just where *he* has planned. Our spiritual gifts have been dispensed by *his* hands. And so, when we have done all that God has prepared for us to do, let us be sure that *he* gets the praise!

Amen, Aquila! Thanks be to God!

Reflect on these points

1. *Every church and minister needs multiple gospel partners: multiple Priscillas and Aquilas. Think about your church. Where do you fit in? How and where do the leaders need you?*

2. *Do you consider correction a blessing? Has anyone ever attempted to help you as Priscilla and Aquila helped Apollos? How did you receive them? Is there still listening to be done?*

3. *Consider the unusual and difficult circumstances that brought Paul together with two of the greatest gospel partners he ever had. Keep their plight—and God's good providence—in mind the next time you are faced with unwanted circumstances. If you are his, God will work all things together for your good as assuredly as he did for Priscilla and Aquila!*

# Epaphras:
## The small-town
## church-planter

*Epaphras, who is one of your number, a bondslave of Jesus Christ, sends you his greetings, always laboring earnestly for you in his prayers, that you may stand perfect and fully assured in all the will of God. For I testify for him that he has a deep concern for you and for those who are in Laodicea and Hierapolis.*

*(Col. 4:12–13)*

Epaphras is mentioned only three times in the New Testament. In Colossians 1 we learn that it was he who brought the good news of Jesus to the town of Colossae. They 'learned it from Epaphras, our beloved fellow bond-servant', the apostle Paul wrote in verse 7. In Philemon 23 we discover that this same Epaphras was later imprisoned with the apostle for the sake of that good news. And in Colossians 4 (above) we are informed that, even while in prison, the founding pastor of the church at Colossae continued to minister to his beloved flock by means of earnest, hard-working prayer!

So the man we consider in this chapter was remarkable indeed—a missionary/pastor; a sufferer for Jesus' sake; and a man of deep love and relentless prayer. I want to know more about a man like that—and surely you do too. But the Bible says so little about Epaphras that, if we want to piece together the puzzle of his *life*, we have to sort through the history of *the church* which he planted and of *the people* to whom he ministered. By learning their story, we better understand his.

So who were these people who (Col. 1:7) 'learned [the gospel] from Epaphras', and for whom (Col. 4:12) he laboured earnestly in prayer? And what do the answers to those questions tell us about the man who preached to the Colossians and cared for their souls?

Colossae was a relatively inconsequential town in Asia Minor located in the Lycus River valley, situated in what is today the nation of Turkey. Indeed, it was 'a small town', we are told by one ancient geographer.[1] Its place in the pecking order of Asia Minor's cities is perhaps underscored by the fact that Paul himself, though he travelled nearby, seems not to have focused any of his own personal missionary efforts on Colossae.[2] He had 'heard of' the Colossians' faith (Col. 1:4), but had apparently never met them in person (2:1). So Colossae was, as far as the first century was concerned, what we might call a bit of a backwater. And even today, despite the town's place in biblical history, its ruins have never been excavated by archaeologists.[3]

Far from being the kind of bustling urban centre where so many young ministers want to plant new churches, being assigned as the missionary pastor to Colossae would have been more akin to starting a church in a little river town a few hours outside the big city! Perhaps you know of a small city just like that in a locality near you—maybe not a dead-end street, but perhaps not a prime place for growing a big church either. But a man named Epaphras was apparently humble enough to take the job.

How did it happen? During his third missionary journey, the apostle Paul spent about three years in the great city of

Ephesus (in the same region of Asia Minor in which little Colossae was situated). Given Ephesus's importance, Paul naturally wanted to gain a foothold for the gospel in that city.[4] But his focus seems not to have been on Ephesus *exclusively*. For in Colossians 1:7, when Paul refers to Epaphras's ministry among the people of Colossae, he speaks of him as serving Christ 'on our behalf'. Evidently, Epaphras began his mission to Colossae at least with Paul's blessing, and quite possibly as Paul's emissary—sent out with the gospel, on Paul's behalf, from the metropolis of Ephesus to the much more modest mission field of Colossae.[5] Further, the fact that Paul calls Epaphras 'one of your number' in Colossians 4:12 may be an indication that Epaphras was originally *from* Colossae. And he was the man to go now and proclaim the gospel to this little borough.

So, when the assignment came, Epaphras left the grand city of Ephesus and the important and influential church there. He left the opportunity of hearing the great apostle preach on a weekly basis. And he went (or perhaps went *back*) to little old Colossae. Colossians 4:13 seems to indicate that he did perhaps also work at some point in the more prominent nearby cities of Laodicea and Hierapolis[6]—but he didn't overlook their smaller and less-influential sister city Colossae! And it would appear, from Paul's letter to the church there, that Epaphras succeeded in his task. He preached the gospel, and some of the people in Colossae believed (Col. 1). He then established them into a local congregation. Along the way, he raised up at least one other leader in the church as well (Archippus, 4:17). Then, at some point, he appears to have left the little church in the hands of Archippus and gone to rejoin Paul's missionary team—which is where he was to be found when Paul wrote his letter to the Colossians: in Rome, alongside the apostle— both of them imprisoned for the gospel's sake (Philem. 23). And, having heard from Epaphras of all that God was doing in Colossae, Paul wrote to the church from his prison cell to encourage them in the Lord (providing a brief greeting and update from their beloved former church-planter as well).

That is Epaphras's story as far as we know it from the Scriptures—and there are great encouragements to be drawn from his life and labours on behalf of the Colossian church. The first such is gleaned, not directly from Epaphras's own character, but from the context in which he ministered. So, along those lines, let us think about ...

### The worth of small churches

We have already seen that the church in Colossae was located in a small *town*. But it was probably also a small *church*. Epaphras would have had very little in the way of numbers about which to brag at the local ministers' meetings! How do I know that? Because, in Philemon 2, we learn that the church in Colossae met in a house. So the numbers of people coming every Sunday couldn't have been all that large—even if the people were crammed in to the rafters. Incidentally, this seems to have been true of many churches in those early days.

Specifically, the church at Colossae met in the house of a

slave-owner named Philemon, who Paul was concerned might have trouble forgiving a runaway called Onesimus. And it was apparently this home-owner's son, Archippus (Philem. 2), who took over as pastor of the church when Epaphras's work among them was complete (Col. 4:17).

So let's just review the church at Colossae for a moment or two. The town itself was only a small blip on the radar screen. The church, after perhaps several years of existence, was still small enough to be meeting in a private home. The owner of that home was evidently a sincere Christian, but also having trouble with a runaway slave. Their pastor was the son of the home-owner. And their former pastor was in prison!

That does not sound like the most 'happening' place in the world, does it? It does not sound like a sophisticated, suburban megachurch. Rather, it sounds more like a tiny little hodge-podge of no-names and strugglers—like most small churches today! And yet they were important enough for God to have sent his only begotten Son into the world to live perfectly on their behalf, and to die for their sins! They were worthwhile enough for Paul to have sent a missionary to them! They were valuable enough for Epaphras to have given his valuable time, effort, and prayers in their service! And the Spirit had done enough good in these men and women that Paul could call them 'saints and faithful brethren' (Col. 1:2)!

So what is the lesson of Colossae, and of Epaphras's faithful but obscure labours in that small town? God does not measure success in terms of numbers, renown, or grand achievements.

Therefore it is more important to be saintly than to be slick; more vital to be faithful than to be fast-paced; more imperative that a church exhibit *grace* in its members than be able to boast of fantastic *growth* in its roster!

The strength of a church is not in its sophistication—and not necessarily in its numbers either. Yes, we surely want to see God saving souls and adding them to our churches 'day by day', as he did at Jerusalem in Acts 2. But it is imperative that we notice that God did not work in exactly the same way in Colossae as he did in Jerusalem. Yet the church in Colossae was still called 'faithful' (Col. 1:2). And Paul could still praise this little church because the gospel was indeed 'bearing fruit and increasing' (1:6), albeit not at the same pace as in the congregation in the Jewish capital! Hopefully, the same could be said of *your* congregation, even if it is not all that glamorous a gathering of folk; and even if, in a pinch, you could squeeze the whole lot into your living room!

The strength of a church is not in its size or in its sophistication, but in whether or not it is filled with 'saints and faithful brethren'. So we should take heart, and make it our aim to be as saintly and faithful as we possibly can be! And, secondly, like the apostle Paul did on behalf of Epaphras, we should take note of …

### The praiseworthiness of pioneer missionaries

That is what Epaphras was—a pioneer missionary. He went—as was always Paul's goal as well—where Christ had not yet been named. He went to a place that evidently had no churches, no other missionaries, and no access to the gospel. We know that because Paul tells us in Colossians 1:7 that the Colossians learned the gospel from Epaphras. Evidently, no one else had been there with the good news before. Or if they had, the gospel had not taken root previously.

Epaphras went into virgin territory. And, in order to do so, he had to bury himself in relative obscurity. If Colossae was, indeed, his hometown (4:12), the task may have been a little bit easier for him. But still, no one was going to hear very much about what he was doing way out in Colossae. His preaching was not going to become renowned, no matter how solid or eloquent it may have been. Yet Epaphras, for the sake of the gospel, chose to go out into a minor burgh, where very few people from the outside world would have the faintest idea of what he was doing; and where, even when people did hear of him, there would be little in the way of numerical success to impress them.

This is the lot in life of almost every pioneer missionary. The very fact that they serve where Christ is not yet named means that there are no large churches in which to make a name for themselves or be thought heroic; no large crowds to be impressed with them; and no appetite for Christian social media outlets through which they might become famous in the world of the evangelical Internet! No, the very idea of becoming a pioneer missionary requires the forfeiture of all these things and the burying of oneself in obscurity for the sake of the gospel, and for the sakes of the people in darkness who need that gospel so badly.

Perhaps you know, or your church supports, a family that has gone into the Muslim world to proclaim Christ. They could be well known, well paid, and involved in a far more 'successful' ministry if they remained at home. But instead they hold services on their living-room floor, in a foreign language, with only a dozen or so people gathered around them—simply in order that they might be faithful to God's calling. And we ought to praise such men and women! Or perhaps you have met an international brother who was saved *out of* that far-off world and came to the West to study theology. But now he has gone back, with his family, to minister in the small, out-of-the-way, Christless little province from which he came. He could have stayed in the Western world with all its comforts, opportunities, and large churches. But he, perhaps like Epaphras, has thought it better to go back home, and to bring light into the darkness from which he came. I say again that we ought to praise such men and women! Whoever they are, and wherever they come from, we ought to join Paul in recognizing the worth of modern-day Epaphrases! We ought to know and tell their stories. And some of us ought to join them out in the middle of nowhere, for Jesus' sake!

But let me ask: Why is this willing self-burial so magnificently praiseworthy? And why ought some of us to join Epaphras and these others in it? Precisely because it is so Christlike! Didn't Jesus bury himself in obscurity in order to bring (and to *be*) the good news to us? To be sure, Jerusalem was no backward city, humanly speaking: it was the capital of the Jewish world. But in comparison with heaven, what was Jerusalem? In comparison with the crowds of angels worshipping around Jesus' throne and praising him night and day, what was a crowd of a few thousand people on the hillsides of Galilee? Quite obscure! And yet Christ left the praise, the perfection, and the adoration! He denied himself, so that he might walk among us *and die in our place.* That is the ultimate in self-burial!

So when a man or woman chooses to go where Christ is not named, where there are no crowds to admire his preaching, and no Christian friends to praise her abilities, and no larger Christian culture in which he or she may shine or be noticed—the pioneer missionary is following not just in the footsteps of Epaphras, but of Jesus!

Epaphras, like so many Bible worthies before him, is a way-marker, pointing us to Jesus by his Christlike example. And now, finally, let me use his example to call your attention to ...

## The labour of earnest prayer

Remember that Paul wrote to the Colossians from prison. Remember also that, according to Philemon 23, Epaphras was there with him. So, while Paul wrote in Colossians 1 of what Epaphras had *already* done for the church at Colossae (teaching them the gospel, v. 7), in Colossians 4 Paul shifted gears and spoke of what Epaphras was *still* doing on their behalf, even from his prison cell. And what was Paul observing there? Epaphras pacing up and down the cell, praying for his little flock in Colossae—'always laboring earnestly for you in his prayers'!

What would *you* pray about in prison? I would pray for my release! But what kinds of words rose from Epaphras's lips as he languished there in the dungeon? 'O God, help my dear friends in Colossae to "stand perfect and fully assured in all the will of God" [v. 12]. Assure them that your plans *will* come to fruition. And show them what your plans *are*! Bless Archippus's preaching and pastoring so that they might know all your will!'

What a prayer! There are several lessons we might glean from it. One is simply that, when we really love someone, our heart will groan for that person in prayer. When we really have 'a deep concern' (4:13) for a brother or sister in Christ, or for a church, we will (4:12) always labour earnestly for that person in prayer. I hope that proves true in your own relationships and prayer life—and in mine.

Epaphras's prayers from the Roman prison also remind us that, sometimes, all we can do is pray. Epaphras was no longer in Colossae. Nor was he free to return there. He could no longer teach, counsel, correct, or encourage his flock. He could no longer be there at the weddings, sickbeds, baptisms, and fellowship meals. But he could still labour on their behalf—in prayer! And the same sorts of things may someday be true of you.

Someday your children will no longer be under your roof.

Someday your loved one will lie on a sickbed, and there will be nothing you can do to make things better. Someday you will be too old or weak to do what you once did—in the family, or for the church. And, in each of those instances, it will be tempting to focus on what you *cannot* do; on the ways in which you can no longer be there for that person; on the ways you were once able to help, but are no longer capable of doing so. Perhaps Epaphras was tempted to think in exactly these ways. But instead of pacing up and down, *fretting* because he was no longer able to teach or be there for his beloved flock, he was pacing up and down the prison block (or was down on his knees) *praying* for them! We must learn a lesson from him. We must remember that, even when there is nothing else we can do, we *can* pray. God is more than capable of intervening, even when our hands are tied!

Notice one final thing about Epaphras's prayer: Paul called it *labour*! Epaphras, he said, is 'always *laboring* earnestly for you in his prayers'. His prayers were an intense 'wrestling' (NIV)—like Jacob with the Lord in Genesis 32. Indeed, perhaps that is precisely what Epaphras was doing in that prison cell—labouring in prayer for the Colossians, and refusing to let God go until he had secured a blessing for his beloved little flock! Oh, that the Lord's people today had such a fervent spirit in prayer!

How vital this is, especially, for ministers! As N. T. Wright points out, Paul's emphasis on the prayerful struggling in which both he (2:1–3) and Epaphras (4:12–13) engaged demonstrates that 'Paul regards prayer as more than just a pious ancillary activity to preaching and teaching: it is part of the work itself'.[7] The apostles in Jerusalem gave prayer the same prominence (Acts 6:4). And so must pastors today! And not only must *pastors* embrace the indispensable role of prayer in the work of the gospel, but so must *everyone* who seeks to serve our Lord. As Oswald Chambers said famously: 'Prayer does not fit us for the greater works; prayer *is* the greater work.'[8] Prayer is just as important as service; just as important as sharing the gospel, preaching a sermon, teaching a class, or working on a church outreach event. Praying for our children is just as important as raising them. Praying for our spouses is just as vital as serving them. And the list could go on …

Without his life-giving and strengthening power, Jesus taught us in John 15, our labours will amount to exactly nothing! So it is not enough simply to *work* hard: we must also *pray* hard! Prayer must not merely be something we do for just a few minutes, before we get down to the *real* business of serving God. No; rather, because we realize that we can do nothing without God's power, praying is just as important as doing! Prayer is part of the labour!

Paul and Epaphras understood this. 'Epaphras', Paul wrote, is 'always laboring earnestly for you in his prayers'. In other words, he didn't stop serving his people when he moved away, or even when he went to prison. Even in absence, he was still hard at work on their behalf—in prayer.

What if we all saw things as Paul, Epaphras, and Oswald

Chambers saw them? What if we all took it to heart that one of the most important labours we can perform on behalf of our churches, families, co-workers, and neighbourhoods is the labour of prayer? There is no telling how faithful and fruitful they (and we) might become!

## Reflect on these points

1. *Is your church relatively small or quirky, like the collection of folk at Colossae? In spite of its size or shortcomings, thank God for the gifts and graces that are indeed present in your local family of believers. And marvel that Jesus shed his blood even for this unusual bunch!*

2. *Think about a missionary family you know—their distance from home, the difficulty of their work, perhaps the slowness of church growth in the region in which they serve. Pray for them. And think about how you might encourage them in the midst of their obscurity.*

3. *Picture Epaphras again—praying hard in his prison cell because he so loved his brothers and sisters in the Lord. What gospel causes or Christian brothers or sisters warrant such fervent prayer from your lips? Pray for them even now.*

# Endnotes

## Introduction

**1** We were actually reading Obadiah's story as retold in Catherine MacKenzie's *Hall of Fame: Old Testament* (Tain: CF4Kids, 2001).

## Ch. 1 Barzillai

**1** Any italicized emphasis given within scriptural quotations is the present author's and is not original to the NASB® text.

## Ch. 2 Obadiah

**1** You can subscribe to this newsletter on their website, www.persecution.com.

**2** In these two sentences about Satan's Jezebels and God's Obadiahs I borrow from a similar line about Satan's Ahab and God's Elijah in the famous sermon 'Payday Someday' by R. G. Lee.

## Ch. 4 Ebed-melech

**1** I learned this point from Paris Reidhead, who made it powerfully in his famous sermon 'Ten Shekels and a Shirt', available at sermonaudio.com.

## Ch. 5 John Mark

**1** From the hymn 'I Need Thee Every Hour' by Annie S. Hawks.

**2** In his sermon series 'Pathway to Freedom', Alistair Begg describes how a jeweller's black velvet cloth sets off the brilliance of a diamond, as an illustration of how the law of God shows us the blackness of our sin so that we might better comprehend the wonder of the good news of Christ. See specifically the sermon 'Good News for Lawbreakers' from Romans 3:20 at truthforlife.org.

## Ch. 6 Priscilla and Aquila

**1** For the dating of Claudius's edict, see Simon J. Kistemaker, *Acts* (New Testament Commentary; Grand Rapids, MI: Baker, 1990), p. 649; and I. Howard Marshall, *Acts* (Tyndale New Testament Commentary; Grand Rapids, MI: Eerdmans, 1980), p. 293.

**2** For Ephesus as the possible destination of Paul's second letter to Timothy, see Kendell H. Easley, *Holman QuickSource Guide to Understanding the Bible* (Nashville: Holman, 2002), p. 335.

**3** William Hendriksen lays out a very helpful summary of this couple's movements, activities, and character in *Romans* (New Testament Commentary; Grand Rapids, MI: Baker, 1980–81), pp. 501–503. I have made use of his material in compiling my own summary.

**4** Ibid, p. 502.

**5** Not only did Paul write that an overseer (i.e. elder or pastor) should be the *husband* of one wife (1 Tim. 3:2), but he also indicated that one of the functions of an elder is teaching—a ministry from which he precluded women in a whole-church context (1 Tim. 2:12).

# Ch. 7 Epaphras

**1** Strabo, *Geography* XII.viii.13, quoted in William Hendriksen, *Colossians and Philemon* (New Testament Commentary; Grand Rapids, MI: Baker, 1964), p. 13.

**2** 'Paul … seems to have concentrated on major centres of population.' N. T. Wright, *Colossians and Philemon* (Tyndale New Testament Commentary; Grand Rapids, MI: Eerdmans, 1986), p. 22.

**3** 'Colossae', Wikipedia, https://en.wikipedia.org/wiki/Colossae, accessed 22 August 2014.

**4** Again, 'Paul … seems to have concentrated on major centres of population.' Wright, *Colossians and Philemon*, p. 22.

**5** Kendell Easley seems to hint at this explanation of events, noting the probability that Epaphras went to Colossae 'from Ephesus', 'while Paul was in Ephesus on his third missionary journey' (*Holman QuickSource Guide*, pp. 311–312). Further, I was helped to notice and understand the significance of the phrase 'on our behalf', and the origins of Epaphras's mission to Colossae, by N. T. Wright's introduction to the book of Colossians and his exposition of 1:7. Epaphras, he points out, 'brought news of Christ *from Paul* to Colossae on his, Paul's, behalf' (my emphasis; *Colossians and Philemon*, pp. 22, 55). From these observations I conclude that Epaphras went to Colossae at the very least with Paul's blessing, and perhaps by Paul's assignment. And from Easley's observations, I conclude that this probably took place during Paul's three-year stay in Ephesus.

**6** For the greater importance of Hierapolis and Laodicea in comparison with Colossae, see Hendriksen, *Colossians and Philemon*, pp. 10 13.

**7** Wright, *Colossians and Philemon*, p. 158.

**8** *My Utmost for His Highest* (Uhrichsville, OH: Barbour & Company, 1997), p. 215.